# Ascension Press

## In Your Holy Spirit:
### Traditional Spiritual Practices in Today's Christian Life

Michelle Heyne

Published by Ascension Press
The Episcopal Resource Center
P.O. Box 1190
Fayetteville, AR 72702

In Your Holy Spirit:
Traditional Spiritual Practices
in Today's Christian Life

Published 2011 by Ascension Press
© Michelle Heyne and Robert Gallagher

We have written two companion books. This is *In Your Holy Spirit: Traditional Spiritual Practices in Today's Christian Life,* which addresses the individual's spiritual practice.

*In Your Holy Spirit: Shaping the Parish Through Spiritual Practice,* by Robert Gallagher, is focused on how the parish church and its clergy can better support and foster the development of spiritual life and practices and in so doing improve the health of the whole parish.

To see more titles from Ascension Press, please visit www.orderoftheascension.org.

For information on congregational development, including training programs, papers, and other resources visit:

www.shapingtheparish.com

www.congregationaldevelopment.com

This book is dedicated to the memory of my father, Paul Heyne, who would have enjoyed arguing with me about what he didn't agree with, and also would have been secretly pleased that the apple didn't fall that far from the tree.

And to the memory of Mary and Carroll Hinderlie, who enfleshed both wonder and joy in the Incarnation and a tangible commitment to the way of the cross. Plus, they were a heck of a lot of fun.

# Contents

*Give them an inquiring and discerning heart, the courage to will and to persevere, a spirit to know and to love you, and the gift of joy and wonder in all your works.*

**The Book of Common Prayer**

# Introduction

The prayer on the facing page is the one offered after a person is baptized with water and before the sealing with oil. This prayer provides a glimpse into what we can become as we grow into our baptismal identity.

In this book, we hope to provide ways in which individual Christians can approach their spiritual lives, to help deepen and further develop them, and to take greater adult responsibility for that development. We will offer some theory, some images, but mainly we will offer concrete ways in which individuals can enter into the mystery of the Holy and better integrate their experience of daily life with the sacred.

We have written two companion books addressing spiritual practices. Michelle Heyne, working with input from Bob Gallagher, has written about spiritual practices from the perspective of the laity. Bob Gallagher, working with input from Michelle, has written about how the parish church and its clergy can better support and foster the development of spiritual life and practices. Both use the same map of spiritual practice.

The "map" we are offering includes five elements. At the base there are two practices—one weekly, one daily. That rhythm is common to many religious and spiritual traditions. These elements have to do with living in the habits and ways that keep us grounded in what is most real. In Anglicanism they take form as the Holy Eucharist (Mass, Communion) and the Daily Office (Divine Office, Liturgy of the Hours, Daily Prayer of the Church).

There are two more elements standing side-by-side on that base—Community and Reflection. Our assumption is that we are all called to be part of not just the broader human and national communities but also of particular, imperfect communities that we allow to nurture and influence us. In Anglicanism that includes the parish church. Reflection includes developing our capacity to be silent and still; to listen to our life; and to learn from our experience. Reflection is about connecting our internal life to the life of God.

The final element is Service. We are all called to serve in ways that fit our gifts and temperament. That service may be most fruitful, for others and for us, when it sits upon the base of the other four spiritual practices.

## Perspective and Approach

I write this as a devout Episcopalian living in Seattle, Washington. I am intellectually-oriented, socially liberal, a feminist, and a Christian deeply committed to the traditional expression of faith found in the Anglican Church[1]. The Northwest is frequently cited as being profoundly "unchurched," and indeed, few of my friends or even family members are involved with any form of organized religion.

At the same time, the Northwest is known as a place of pervasive and extensive spirituality, where, for example, self-identification as "spiritual but not religious" is an absolute must when signing up with on-line dating services or when complaining about the latest excesses of the religious right. As a person who considers herself both spiritual and religious, I am aware of how unusual that idea has become in many circles.

"Spirituality" is a big word and it can mean pretty much anything you want it to. In writing this, I am most drawn to Henri Nouwen's statement that "the spiritual life is a reaching out to our innermost self, to our fellow human beings and to our God." Spirituality is often, but not always, grounded in a specific religious tradition that concretizes the meaning, form, and content of those forms of "reaching out." Religion and its institutions, its communities, ties, traditions, and ways of being, provide us with a structure that can facilitate the transformation of spiritual longing into action.

The further we wander from the traditional spiritual disciplines

---

[1] The term "Episcopal Church" refers to the American branch of the worldwide Anglican Communion—all members of that communion are therefore "Anglicans," regardless of national affiliation or specific nation-based church names. I will use both terms interchangeably when referring to the Episcopal Church and its members.

of the church and its norms around Eucharist, common prayer, and community life, the more likely we are to nurture the sinfulness, egocentricism, and abuse of power that flourish in human institutions. Fights and schisms tend to erupt in response to conflicting understandings of spiritual health, of sin, and of the worthiness of others. Conflict over these issues that grows out of a shared spiritual practice can be quite different from conflicts that arise from our independent assessment of them from a stance of outsider, owner, or arbiter.

I like to imagine that we can see ourselves instead as members of the Body of Christ. Norms, structures, and community life—the content and pattern of our spiritual discipline—all require us to come up against something outside ourselves that is presumed valuable and then decide how to respond to the challenge. Are we absorbed into the machine? Do we fight it? Do we pick and choose, ignoring what we dislike, embracing what we do like? Do we chuck the whole thing whenever it becomes uncomfortable, or even infuriating? The transformation occurs when we accept that we are members of the Body of Christ, and we recognize that the Body is not separate from its members but neither is it the sum of its parts.

My own life has been shaped by the Anglican tradition and, most important, by Anglican worship in community, and I write from that perspective. Religious affiliation is not a mere preference; rather, it is deeply connected to who we are as human beings and how each of us can best enter into a relationship with the divine and be transformed by that relationship. That emphatically does not mean that those who take a different path are wrong or misguided, but it also doesn't mean that every path is equally valid or equally useful.

Many of the practices we will explore in this book have a long history in the Catholic churches and variations are commonly found in Protestant denominations, as well as in other faiths. They do not belong solely to one branch of the church, but they may have a particular flavor or expression depending on the religious community they come out of. Much of what we will talk about can be usefully adapted to a wide range of denominations and worship styles. Examples include the importance of choosing to participate and take responsibility for your own spiritual life; the use of silence in worship; the importance of reflectiveness; how we participate in community; and the nature of Christian service. Some of the specific liturgical actions or administrative structures we describe may be most common in the Episcopal Church, but the underlying ideas are foundational to Christian practice.

While less liturgical traditions will not, for example, have the same experience of Eucharist or Daily Office described in this book, I do think it's worthwhile to consider the nature of worship whatever one's tradition. How does it feed you? How does it aid your encounter of the living God? How does it help you grow up in Christ? This book may offer you approaches or perspectives useful in terms of your stance toward worship and your own internal sense of how you will get what you need, regardless of the form that worship takes around you.

*We were losing the more traditional form of faith which saw religion as a practical activity. Like driving, swimming, dancing or gymnastics, you learn the truths of faith only by constant, dedicated practice—not by reading texts or adopting a metaphysical 'belief'. Like a myth, a religious doctrine is essentially a program of action. It makes no sense unless it is translated into practical action that helps you to dethrone egotism, selfishness and greed by practicing compassion to all living beings.*

**Karen Armstrong**, discussing her book *The Case for God*, *Washington Post web site, October 8, 2009*

# One

# Our Key Assumptions and How to Use this Book

This book, and the companion book for use by parish clergy, is intended for use with just about any regular attendee, including those who have recently started attending on a regular basis. They can provide a base for a parish's incorporation process.

Some of the assumptions we begin with include these:

1.  We all have a spiritual life.

2.  It is a significant act of spiritual growth when we accept responsibility for our spiritual life.

3.  A healthy spiritual life assumes engagement, rather than escape; an interest in the life of the world instead of spiritual sentimentality or being caught up in illusions.

4.  We are seeking a spiritual practice with roots in ancient ways and useful in modern life.

5.  We need a spirituality that is both solid and resilient.

6.  Our spiritual life serves us best when we understand that it is to evolve over time. What serves us when we are 11 differs from when we are 18 and still again from when we are 35 or 60. A fertile evolution unfolds out of forms of spiritual life that are complex, rich, and paradoxical. They continue to grow as we increase our self-awareness, insight, and in response to changing circumstances.

7.  It requires efficiency if it is to serve modern daily life.

8.  It requires attention and time if it is to serve modern daily life.

9.  Our spiritual life and discipline is to be based on an integrated system, a pattern, rather than series of random practices. We are to live our spiritual life by Rule, not rules.

10. It is possible for the average church member to become competent and proficient in spiritual practices.

11. We must decide to base our spiritual life on persistence, courage, and competence, rather than on feelings—whether we feel like praying or not. A useful and faithful spiritual life requires critical reasoning and intelligences. We need to intentionally turn away from spiritual fads and fast food.

12. The parish church's primary task is the spiritual formation of its people.

## How to use this book

There are several ways to approach this book. Each chapter focuses on a different aspect of spiritual practice and examines various ways of entering into these practices. Within a broad category (e.g., Eucharist), there may be sub-sets of things to consider, such as using silence or using the body.

You might experiment with a different chapter each month. You might decide to focus on one area and pick one practice each week. You could brainstorm about spiritual practices you or other church members have experienced and then prioritize by reflecting on what's been helpful and sustainable over time.

You might read the book, or a specific section, with other members of the parish and help one another learn new behaviors or support community changes, such as observing more silence before church starts.

One helpful process for furthering both group discussion and learning is to take a few minutes and write down your own thoughts in response to one of the sections, questions, or specific practices. Then share what you would like to with one or two other people. Finally bring back to the broader group some of what you've shared. Then ask yourselves to name one thing you've learned and one thing you'd like to try.

This book is, above all, meant to be *used*. Try something, reflect on how it goes. Try something else, either on its own or in tandem with what you've already taken on.

We suggest you begin by reviewing the map below and then taking the Spiritual Practices Assessment that appears at the end of this chapter. Taking the assessment may raise questions for you or otherwise provide a direction to your reading.

## A map of spiritual practice

We will repeatedly suggest that a full and rich spiritual life requires actual spiritual practices and the development of actual spiritual discipline. We use the image of a spiritual "map," a broad structure of Weekly Practice (Eucharist); Daily Practice (Office); Reflection; Community; and Service to frame the development of spiritual practice.

A map offers a system of spiritual life rather than a list of assorted practices. A useful system will provide a balance of nurture and stretching. It will include our inner life and our outer life. In such a system our inclinations and gifts are supported and allowed to flourish and the less developed parts of us are drawn out and developed. All so we may become stronger in love and faith; more resilient, with a broader mind and an enlarged heart.

Maps are useful things.

1.  They are based on the experience of many others. This is how others have made the journey.

2.  They help you get somewhere. If you want to grow in the spiritual life it may help to have a guide.

3.  They change as the circumstances of life change. In a world of rapid change and loose ties among people we have an increased need for a sense of perspective, being in community, and engaging daily routines that give us ground to stand upon.

4.  They are only useful if people find them useful. People vary in temperament and spiritual inclination. Maps can provide too much or too little detail for different groups of people. The old maps, whether of 1932 or of 1976, continue to serve those able to embrace them. Our hope is that the map we offer here will serve many people seeking ancient practices to help them effectively and faithfully engage contemporary life.

## A Map: Spiritual Practices

Action

Integration

Grounding

Adoration & Awe Adoration & Awe Adoration & Awe Adoration & Awe Adoration & Awe

### Service

↑   ↑   ↑   ↑   ↑

### Reflection   Community

↑   ↑   ↑   ↑   ↑

### Eucharist   Daily Prayers of the Church

### TRINITY

Life in the community of the Trinity

A state of being entered into at baptism. God: beyond us, beside us, within us.

*The unifying of the personality, the integration of mind and heart into one center* (Leech)

*My life shall be a real life, being wholly full of Thee.* (St. Augustine)

*The end ... would be a commonwealth of free, responsible beings united in love* (John Macquarrie)

We are aware that one impediment to a disciplined spiritual life is the soul-deadening tendency some of us have to focus obsessively on the rules and on what we "should" do, as well as our abiding suspicion that the only really valid expressions of the holy involve a lot of boredom, suffering, and priggishness. What a shock we don't jump right in!

A rule-based approach to the spiritual life may tend to perpetuate a sense of false duality, rather than supporting us in engaging the complex polarities to be managed. Many points of conflict around significant life issues will remain sources of tension and are not amendable to a particular "solution" or to otherwise being resolved. The classic example of a polarity is breathing: we take oxygen in when we inhale, and we release carbon dioxide when we exhale. Both are necessary functions and each relies on the other.

Getting stuck in one end of the cycle (e.g., breathing out without then breathing in) means death. No one would ever talk about "needing to resolve the problem of whether to breathe in or out," but we may be perfectly comfortable talking about whether we connect to the tradition *or* we innovate, whether we engage stability *or* change, and whether we join the church *or* hold onto our personal spiritual values.

Just as it is possible to become too rigid and dogmatic about what we're "supposed to do," it is possible to over-react to perceived pressure from the rules or the "shoulds," rejecting out of hand the wisdom of tradition, the authority of community, or the system of spiritual discipline.

Excessive concern about losing our identity may prevent us from consciously committing to anything bigger than ourselves, yet we will, in innumerable ways, spend our whole lives working out the complexities of belonging, of identity, of connection. Who am I? What will this cost me? What is my duty to others? Will they want what I have to offer? What can I expect from them? How much will they accept from me?

The process of spiritual maturation involves openness to exactly those complexities and acceptance that "resolution," if it ever comes, is part of our eternal, not our temporal, inheritance.

> We can…[entertain] the notion that one might grow into faith much as one writes a poem. It takes time, patience, discipline, a listening heart. There is precious little certainty, and often great struggling, but also joy in our discoveries. The joy we experience, however, is not visible or quantifiable; we have only the words and form of the poem, the results of our exploration. Later, the thinkers and definers come along and treat these results as the whole—*Let's see; here she's used a metaphor, and look, she's made up a rhyme scheme. Let's stick with it. Let's teach it. Let's make it a rule.* What began as an experiment, a form of play, an attempt to engage in dialogue with mystery, is now a dogma, set in stone." Kathleen Norris, *The Cloister Walk*

We hope you will come away from this book with awareness of new choices, with a greater sense of competence in and responsibility for your own spiritual life, and also with a greater confidence that the spiritual can be infused with the creative, informed by an experimental stance, and by hope in both God's mercy and his sense of humor.

## Assessing Your Spiritual Practices

### SUNDAY EUCHARIST

**1. Attendance** (circle one)

| Almost Never | About ¼ of the Time | Half the Time | ¾ of the Time | Almost every Sunday |
|---|---|---|---|---|

**2. My ability to participate** (Circle the number that is closest to your experience)

| I am frequently confused and uncertain about how to participate | | | | I can "flow" with it. I mostly don't need a Prayer Book or leaflet. |
|---|---|---|---|---|
| 1 | 2 | 3 | 4 | 5 |

### PARTICIPATING IN THE DAILY PRAYERS OF THE CHURCH

**3. Saying the Office.** I say the Office in some form on my own or with others.

| Never | Only when offered at a meeting or retreat | Sporadically or during some season(s) of the church year | Most days |
|---|---|---|---|

**4. Knowing how** to do the Daily Office.

| I have no idea. | | | I understand how to use it in the Prayer Book and ways to innovate the use |
|---|---|---|---|
| 1 | 2 | 3 | 4 | 5 |

## Disciplined Ways of Reflecting ["Listen to your life"]

Grounding/centering yourself so you can reflect. The spiritual practice of "pondering" and seeking God's presence in the people, circumstances and things of life. Practices that connect daily life to God.

### 5. Ways that work for me

| I don't have ways that work for me | | | I have ways that are effective for me |
|---|---|---|---|
| 1 | 2 | 3 | 4 | 5 |

## Participating in the Parish Community

**6. The community I seek** is one in which people are free to be themselves; to speak and listen fully and authentically. In which differences are accepted (we can fight with those we love). In which we can make decisions and solve the problems we face.

| I don't want church to be that way | | | It is what I seek and more |
|---|---|---|---|
| 1 | 2 | 3 | 4 | 5 |

### 7. Connection with people

| I don't know anyone well | | | I know a number of people and have a few friends in the parish |
|---|---|---|---|
| 1 | 2 | 3 | 4 | 5 |

## 8. Participation in parish social life

| Not at all | | | I participate regularly and frequently |
|---|---|---|---|---|
| 1 | 2 | 3 | 4 | 5 |

**SERVICE**

## 9. In Daily Life—with family & friends, at work, in civic life, and at church.

| I don't have a clear understanding of how I serve in my daily life | | | I am very clear about serving in daily life |
|---|---|---|---|---|
| 1 | 2 | 3 | 4 | 5 |

**THE PROCESS OF SPIRITUAL GROWTH**

## 10. Foundations

| I have a poor foundation in the spiritual practices of the church | | | I have a strong foundation in the spiritual practices of the church |
|---|---|---|---|---|
| 1 | 2 | 3 | 4 | 5 |

## 11. Experiment

| I don't know how or feel confident enough to experiment with spiritual practices | | | I have a sense of how to innovate and experiment with spiritual practices. |
|---|---|---|---|---|
| 1 | 2 | 3 | 4 | 5 |

*For the fully Christian life is a Eucharistic life: that is, a natural life conformed to the pattern of Jesus, given in its wholeness to God, laid on his altar as a sacrifice of love, and consecrated, transformed by his inpouring life, to be used to give life and food to other souls.*

**Evelyn Underhill**

*Just do it.*

**Nike ad campaign**

## My Rule of Life

_____ Morning Prayer

_____ Personal Prayer Period

_____ Meditation

_____ Bible reading and study*

_____ Review the decalogue (p. 350, BCP)

_____ Books/tapes of spiritual formation*

_____ Exhortation to communion (pp. 316f., BCP)

_____ Holy Communion

_____ Altar visit(s)

_____ Examination of conscience/Litany of Penitence (pp. 267ff., BCP)

_____ Reconciliation of a Penitent [(Confession) – pp. 447ff, BCP]

_____ Renewal of baptismal covenant(pp. 304f., BCP)

_____ Spiritual direction

_____ Listening to Christian radio

_____ Meeting with neighborhood "cell" group or catechumenal process group

_____ Apostolic action**

_____ Ministry***

_____ Night prayers

# Two

# The Weekly Practice:
# Holy Eucharist

## Does going to church really matter?

There are places in the country—mainly the South, chunks of the Midwest, parts of the East Coast—where church attendance on Sunday morning is simply what happens. In the West, though, church attendance is more likely to be seen as either entirely optional or an idiosyncratic expression of excessive religiosity. And despite the fact that the US population remains strongly religious overall, there is sometimes a tendency to be suspicious of religious norms that assume the importance of something beyond the individual's personal relationship with God.

Even among regular church-goers, it is relatively rare to hear from the clergy or the laity a direct statement that weekly attendance (regardless of competition from soccer practice, a warm bed, or the Sunday *New York Times*) is both the basic expectation for practicing Christians and of inherent value.

Of course, hectoring people about what they "should" do is seldom useful, but it is also not useful to continue to assume that we all have a shared set of assumptions about spiritual life and spiritual practice and that we all make our choices to participate or not participate from a position of common knowledge and experience.

Even when we are nominally members of the same church, widely divergent generational, socio-economic, and geographical considerations come into play. And our religious diversity exists within a broader culture that increasingly assumes individual preferences and desires should trump communal ones, a development that has had enormous and highly complex impact on modern life. This context means that we are unlikely to automatically draw the same conclusions from shared experiences of worship.

I was raised in a liberal Lutheran-cum-Episcopalian family. Debating was central to our lives—we regularly argued over many political, religious, and intellectual issues at the dinner table. We also went to church on Sundays. I hated it and there was no option, no discussion. A modest amount of whining was tolerated, but that was it.

When I was old enough to control my own destiny, I promptly eliminated church attendance from my schedule. I also made passionate and self-righteous proclamations to my father (who was both an ordained Lutheran minister and an Economics professor) about my personal relationship with God and how I didn't need to "listen to a lot of canned prayers and hang around with hypocrites to communicate with God."

My father, a fine teacher known for his ability to deeply engage with students who disagreed with him, scoffed at me and said baldly, "There's no such thing as Christianity separate from the Christian community." I of course responded to this with great maturity (the memory is a little hazy, but I have vague recollections that I might have accused him of bigotry, ignorance, and closed-mindedness). We spent little additional time on the topic but his remark stuck with me and some part of me suspected that he might be right, even if it was expressed a skosh insensitively.

Imagine my surprise when, a number of years later, I had started going to an Episcopal church in the hope of securing a pretty location in which to get married and picked up a copy of John M. Krumm's *Why Choose the Episcopal Church?* I thought it was a wonderful description of Anglicanism's unique gifts and then I came across this:

> Anglicanism has always insisted that the life of the church and her sacraments must be thought of as necessary "means of grace." Church life is not an elective which a Christian may take on out of a sense of duty and responsibility but may omit without serious damage to his faith. The fact is he cannot

really be a Christian apart from involvement in the community of believers.

I was noticing a theme. I also noticed the fact that just about every Christian leader, from Rick Warren to the Pope, presumed the value of regular church attendance. Still, though, I only went to church when I felt like it, which was admittedly more frequently than it had been when I was a teenager. It was not, though, until my marriage had failed and I was feeling lonely and adrift, that I ventured into the parish with anything approaching regularity. And even then, the real reason I went every week was because I had a crush on another parishioner and the only time I had any chance of seeing him was on Sunday mornings.

The crush went nowhere but an interesting thing happened in my own spiritual life. The practice of showing up, of recognizing that I was part of something bigger than myself, that my presence or absence affected the community, and that the Eucharistic community came together regardless of transitory feeling, profoundly changed my spiritual orientation. I shifted from an assumption that religious observation was an obligation I took on to make me feel better, to an understanding that religious practice was a natural and joyful response to the love of God and the command to love others as he loved us.

## Deciding to join the community

The tradition of the church is that, barring illness or emergency, we will attend the Eucharist every week. For most people, that means one of the Sunday services. For others, though, it may mean some other Eucharist held during the week. We need that regular opportunity to come together as a worshipping community, to be renewed, to be fed with the spiritual food, and to be sent into the world to do the work we have been given to do.

The first step, then, is making a decision to join that Eucharistic community, week in and week out, regardless of how we feel at the time. We need to allow ourselves to enter into the rhythm of the Eucharist and let that rhythm form a kind of backbone to our lives. This will have a transforming effect on its own, but there are also a number of different ways we can individually enter into the Eucharist that affect our receptivity to God, others, and ourselves.

## Competence in participation

Feeling competent at what we do is critical to being able to enjoy our activities, to relax, and to go deeper or otherwise advance our skills.

Think back to when you first learned to drive—so many different parts had to be managed simultaneously, including knowing how to brake, steer, accelerate, shift, when to check the mirrors, determine the appropriate turning radius, how much space to occupy in the lane. Then, on top of the mechanical issues involved in making the car move, you have to carefully monitor the environment—who is near you, who is turning into your lane, stopping ahead of you, accelerating behind you. You have to carefully assess the rate of speed of the traffic around you and how you fit into that.

Even if you were excited about learning to drive, the sheer unfamiliarity with so many moving, interactive parts was inherently stressful. Enjoying the scenery, the people with you in the car, an opportunity to be alone—it would be quite difficult to enter comfortably into these aspects of the drive until you had mastered the primary skills. Eventually, though, while you must maintain concentration and focus, your awareness of the many activities you are successfully juggling recedes to the background and driving becomes much more effortless.

Competence in worship isn't that different (with the significant exception that "mistakes" in worship won't kill you or anyone else, however temporarily embarrassing they may feel) but unfortunately in many parishes we don't get a lot of support for developing competence. We know what competent driving looks like, but we don't get as much information about what competent participation in worship looks like.

There can also be some confusion in the parish about how to best welcome newcomers while recognizing that they may not know how to participate. A mostly non-practicing friend of mine came to a mid-week service with me. This was typically attended by a small group of five or six people, all of whom knew the service by heart.

When the priest recognized that my friend was not familiar with the order of worship, she started giving instructions about what to do or what page to turn to. She also pointedly waited several times while my friend shuffled through the Prayer Book, rather than allowing him to experience the natural rhythm and grace of the service.

My friend's reaction was both discomfort that he was the focus of attention due to his inexperience, and also surprise and a little frustration. As he said, "I'm coming to your church because I figure you guys know something I don't. Why direct the service to my level? How will I learn by doing that?"

The priest was genuinely trying to be helpful but the impact of her behavior did not match her intentions. I think that's connected to the fact that we have few methods for helping people learn while also allowing them to experience worship at its best. We may also assume that people don't have a willingness to learn and that an initial challenge in participation will act as a barrier to joining the church.

Rather than assuming there is a single answer, it seems more helpful to manage the process, take responsibility for our own experience, and to recognize several values that are all true at once.

We all need to feel welcomed and accepted, and we each need to understand that it is OK—inevitable, actually—to be on a learning curve when we first start going to church somewhere.

We also need to experience graceful, dignified, holy worship in a competent Eucharistic community.

Finally, we need opportunities for orientation and building skills. We will build competence when all these factors are attended to, rather than thinking that they are mutually exclusive or that one of them resolves the "problem."

## Building Your Own Sense of Competence

❑ Show up. Trust that simply being present is the first and most important step.

❑ Choose to participate. Recognize that your active role in the congregation is as valuable as the roles of the altar party, even if not as visible. See yourself in the active liturgical role of Worshipper, rather than in the passive role of observer or audience for a performance.

❑ Become familiar with the services you attend.[2] Read through the Prayer Book or the service leaflet outside of worship and notice the structure and order, the choices that are made, the content of the prayers. Check out the rubrics (the italicized comments interspersed throughout the various services) for additional directions, options, and sometimes clarifications.

❑ Experiment with not reading along or holding anything in your hand during the service. Instead of focusing on what you're doing, let the congregation carry you in worship. If you know the service by heart, you may find that different parts catch your attention or you hear the prayers in a new way. Or, you may be surprised to learn how familiar you are with the prayers and other aspects of the service. On the other hand, you may know very little but stepping back may give you some space to learn organically and to worry less about "getting it right." This is similar to learning a language by immersion—it's a tried-and-true method.

❑ Are there aspects of the service you've always had questions about? Why do we do that? When are we supposed to do this? Talk with someone in the parish who might know or who might know where to find out. You may find that others have similar questions and would value the chance to talk.

---

[2] You may find it useful to read *Eucharistic Spirituality: From Audience to Congregation,* Robert A. Gallagher, Ascension Press, 2011.

## PREPARATION

Participation in worship can be enhanced when we allow ourselves to enter into a different space and time. It can be helpful to center yourself when you first come to church through prayer or focused breathing. You might want to read the lessons for the day before the service starts, and then allow yourself to listen to them (rather than reading them) during the service.

❑ Get to church a little early so you don't feel rushed.

❑ Allow yourself a brief time of silence when you first arrive. Consciously enter into a sacred time and a sacred space. This may be a time to avoid chatting with others.

❑ Assume a posture that helps you feel centered. This will differ for people. Some kneel and pray. Some sit and close their eyes. Some carefully notice the environment, the other members of the community.

❑ Prepare for going back into the world by being truly present during worship. Allow yourself to see worship as key to your renewal of baptismal identity, as critical to re-connecting with yourself and your reliance on God. This will help you enter more fully into your daily life, and the ways in which you live your faith organically with family and friends, at work, in civic life, and in the church community.

*At the very least, they can be persuaded that the bodily posture makes no difference to their prayers; for they constantly forget, what you must always remember, that they are animals and that whatever their bodies do affects their souls.*

**C.S. Lewis, *The Screwtape Letters***


*There is a religious underpinning to life, a purpose to everything, an end when all things will work out. Therefore, everything in life points to the center, to Christ the Creator and Redeemer in whom all things—visible and invisible—find their meaning. That's sacrament in its broadest sense.*

*As an Evangelical, I already believed this. I simply had not recognized that this was a sacramental view of life. Now I had a name for it.*

**Robert E. Webber, *Evangelicals on the Canterbury Trail***

## Use of the body

Use of the body is an integral part of liturgical worship. While we may easily understand the concept of sacraments as "outward and visible signs of an inward and spiritual grace," and therefore accept the use of physical elements such as bread and wine, water and oil, our own physicality in worship can seem awkward or unnecessary.

It is, though, a significant method of grounding spiritual life in the whole person—not just in the head or heart. We stand, kneel, sit. We pray silently and aloud. We pray responsively. We listen and we are silent. We sing, we eat and drink. We smell incense or the scent of a snuffed candle wick. We look toward the liturgical action. Bringing our bodies into worship is an important and concrete connection with the Incarnation.

Other physical practices are also common in Episcopal churches. Many bow or genuflect toward the altar when entering or leaving the pew. It is also fairly common to see parishioners bow at the cross in procession.

Less common, but still seen in some churches, is the practice of dipping a hand in the baptismal font and crossing ourselves when entering or leaving the church. There are a number of places in the liturgy when we may cross ourselves as a way of recalling our baptism. Occasionally, you may see someone in the pews bow or genuflect during the Nicene Creed when we say "by the power of the Holy Spirit he became incarnate from the Virgin Mary and was made man."

Our physical actions become a way of expressing our adoration and awe during the many times words fail us or are inadequate in naming the mystery that is God.

In my own parish, there is almost no kneeling at the 10:30 service. In reflecting on my experience, I realized that I missed the particular sense of humility that comes from kneeling during the Confession and I began incorporating that into my practice. I find it helpful, but I don't believe that everyone else should do the same thing. To me, it's a clear example of the importance of parishioners having developed their own sense of liturgical logic and the formative impact of worship, and then feeling free to experiment to find what works for them, in the broader context of the entire Eucharistic community.

## WAYS TO EXPERIMENT WITH USE OF THE BODY

- ❑ Consider changing where you sit. Your sense of comfort and degree of participation can be greatly affected by where you are in the church, whom you sit near, whether you can see and hear[3]. Notice how different locations help or hinder your participation. For example, I've noticed that while I am mostly more comfortable sitting in the back of the church, I also feel more rushed following communion since the service picks up again almost immediately after I return to my pew.

- ❑ Physically turn toward the liturgical action, paying attention with your stance, your eyes, your ears. Look at the deacon and listen while he or she reads the Gospel, rather than reading along in your bulletin. Tune in to rhythm, noticing your movements and responses in the context of both the liturgy and the rest of the congregation.

- ❑ Commit to trying something new for the duration of the service or for several weeks. Examples are crossing yourself, genuflecting, a simple bow when the crucifix passes in procession. Reflect on how it felt and what it was like for you. Try it again and reflect again.

---

[3] As the mother of a young child, I usually sat in the back because I felt self-conscious when my son would make noise or squirm. Those times I sat up-front, though, I realized that Chace was able to actually engage what was going on because he could see it! He was much less restless and much more focused, and also seemed more aware of the people around him.

*The human body and mind need silence, as the monks recognized when they ordered their prayer lives. It is impossible for our inner selves to be prepared to be open to God and receptive to God's Word until we silence our sinful selves—our efforts to be in control, to manipulate everything and everyone to accomplish our own purposes. How can we release ourselves totally to God's Spirit? How can we relinquish our desires to God's better purposes? We need the channel of silence to transport us from the busy harbors of our tensions out to the ocean of God's infinite being.*

**Marva Dawn,** ***Reaching Out Without Dumbing Down***

## Stillness and silence, unhurriedness

We are bombarded by noise in virtually every aspect of our lives. TV, talking, cell phones, the car radio, our Ipod—ubiquitous sound is simply a given, and this sometimes extends to worship. In some parishes, it may even be assumed that periods of silence during worship mean that someone screwed up. With any luck, somebody else will swoop in soon to correct the error and fill the uncomfortable silence with sound, whether a prayer, announcement, or music.

Developing a capacity for silence and stillness, in all places and times, is a foundational skill in the spiritual traditions of Christianity and of other faiths. Though as Norvene Vest explains in *No Moment too Small*, "Strangely enough, we moderns, who experience so little silence, often think that silence is easy. We who are so noise-addicted believe that silence is something anyone can claim readily—until we try it. Being silent is an art to be learned, much like playing baseball or speaking a language."

Feeling hurried is related to discomfort with silence or with stillness (physical silence). Silence may feel passive and we rush through it to get back to "real" activity or "real" worship. It may be helpful to think about "making silence" in the same way we "make noise." Both can be active and intentional.

## WAYS TO EXPERIMENT WITH STILLNESS, SILENCE, AND UNHURRIEDNESS

❑ Focus first on your own physical silence, which is stillness. Allow yourself to sink into your seat, to feel your feet on the ground, to notice where your body is in the space. Make yourself comfortable so you can better avoid fidgeting or shifting uneasily.

❑ Set down papers and books. In corporate worship, the most common interference with silence is the rustling created as we worry about what's coming next and fuss with the hymnal or the leaflet.

❑ Look for opportunities to create silence, starting with refraining from filling silences that may emerge with your own sounds. Intentionally engage the silence and see what happens.

❑ Focus on your breathing. Consider other methods of centering, such as a repetitive prayer or phrase.

❑ Notice distracting thoughts and feelings, tension or anxiety. Let these feelings and thoughts enter your awareness and let them depart.

❑ Create an intention around various parts of the service and engage them, unhurriedly, with that intention in mind. For example, instead of standing during the Offertory because you're eager to get to the main event, consider standing as a physical representation of what you are offering to God, what you carry on your heart, what part of you might be broken and laid on the altar.

❑ Experiment with pacing yourself in relationship to what is going on around you. Listen to the rhythm of the community's prayer and bring yourself into alignment with that rhythm, rather than trying to make the community adopt your pace. Participate in the liturgical action until it's done. For instance, if you're singing a hymn, continue to hold the hymnal and sing the text until the hymn is finished rather than setting the hymnal down in the middle of the last verse. Stand, sit, or pray in *response* to a liturgical action rather than in *anticipation* of a liturgical action.

## Engaging with and listening to the word

Central to liturgical worship is that it is structured and defined and proceeds on its own terms, regardless of our individual preferences. We hear the Bible readings assigned for the day—the same readings that are read in the Church around the world—rather than the readings we're drawn to. The Prayers are arranged to cover a range of concerns that may or may not speak to us on any given day. We recite the Nicene Creed, a sometimes uncomfortably concrete and comprehensive expression of the faith.

Liturgical worship is, at its core, a form of surrender to something bigger than ourselves that we don't control and which is not dependent on our feelings. It does, though, help us participate in a coherent expression of our best feelings, our best intentions, our best efforts to use the human tools of words and action to enter into the presence of God.

But we are human and our desire for "the best" in ourselves and others does not always pan out. Sermons are frequently less than great, and may even be terrible. Bible readings can be boring, disturbing, infuriating, or simply confusing. The Prayers of the People may be read too quietly, too quickly or by someone with limited skill. There's very little we can do to control the content or style of what we hear in church, but there is much we can do about our responses and about the stance we take in listening and engaging what we hear.

The first thing we can do is give ourselves a break. Continuous, focused attention is not always possible or even desirable. If you find your mind wandering, be gentle with yourself and open to the possibility that wandering allows you to be carried into the heart and mind of God. Perhaps it makes sense to bring your attention back to what you're "supposed" to be listening to.

Or maybe what appears to be a distraction is what you need to attend to—something left undone, some invitation to gain new understanding, to accept forgiveness, to comfort your child. If we worship with the assumption that we are responsible for our experience—it's not a performance designed to entertain us—we can engage the experience differently and take from it what is offered.

Many of us get all twisted up over the Bible. We may focus on literal interpretation and immediately move to judgment of ourselves and others or even of the writers of the Bible because we're so irritated that they would think that! Or we simply ignore it, dismissing the Bible as quaint but irrelevant. Most Anglicans derive their familiarity with the Bible largely from hearing it read in worship, rather than through individual study. For some, it is easier to engage liturgically because it can be approached more experientially and less analytically.

Like many modern types, I have found it helpful to study the Bible as a collection of historical documents, written by particular human beings at specific times and from particular cultures. Yet I also see the writers of the Bible as the bearers of the faith, wrestling with the mess and confusion and fear inherent in encountering the living God, trying to discern his mind, and to live into his promise.

The immediacy, passion, and urgency of so much of the Bible is a tremendous gift as I try to connect to those who have gone before and to see what I am called to do today. When I consider what it means to engage the Bible seriously, I assume it means that I must engage it on many levels—emotional, intellectual, with cultural awareness, awe, a sense of mystery, and most important open to how I might be transformed by the encounter.

The Creeds are also a stumbling block for many. Recognizing that the Creeds are the *Church's* statement of faith, not our personal statement of faith, is an important step. The Nicene Creed—the summary of the faith said on Sundays and major feasts—is typically said (or sung) using the word "we," not "I." "We believe," not "I believe."

Accepting the corporate nature of Christian worship and being curious about what it has to say to us as individuals does not mean that we abandon our own beliefs and convictions, but it does mean that we allow ourselves to be shaped by the tradition instead of assuming that it is our job to resist or redefine it.

## WAYS TO EXPERIMENT WITH ENGAGING THE WORD

❑ Set down your papers and look at the lector when the lessons are being read. The lessons in worship are not a form of Bible study; they are part of the liturgy. Most churches today have a Gospel procession, and the Gospel is read from the center of the church. Everyone turns to face the deacon, but in many churches a number of parishioners are staring at the service leaflet, at the text of the Gospel, rather than looking at and listening to the reader.

❑ Consider reading the lessons ahead of time, either at home or perhaps as a form of preparation when you arrive. They're also widely available on the web, either as the Revised Common Lectionary or the Prayer Book Lectionary.

❑ Consider a method of reading Scripture based on the tradition of *lectio divina*. This method assumes God may speak to us in the meditative reading of Scripture. Begin by praying for openness and illumination. Be silent for a few moments, placing yourself in the presence of God. Read one of the readings for the day. Read slowly and meditatively. Allow the words to echo in your mind. Pause briefly for reflection at a few points in your reading. When you are done offer a brief thanksgiving.

❑ Adopt a stance of curiosity and openness. Assume that God has a word for you in today's worship. I can certainly be quite critical of sermons, or the way a lector reads, or the content of a particular passage from the Bible. But instead of nourishing that critic, I can consciously shift my focus and my stance and look for what God may be saying to me.

❑ Let a particular word or phrase grab you. You might find yourself noticing a relationship between the reading or the sermon and whatever you are carrying on your heart in today's Eucharist.

❑ Be aware of your feelings and reactions and consider responding with curiosity rather than judgment. For instance, if you find yourself angry about something in the sermon, refrain from either telling yourself to be more Christian or simply dismissing what you're hearing. Instead, ask what your anger might be telling you. Is there something behind the anger, such as sadness or fear? What does it mean if you and the priest have different standards or perspectives? If your views seem out of synch with the Biblical message you're hearing?

❑ Be open to the challenges that might arise for you in taking seriously the authority of Scripture, reason and tradition, including the spiritual authority of the priest and the Church. How do you maintain your own sense of integrity while being open to a broader tradition and a broader community? Will you allow yourself to be influenced by others as well as wanting to influence them?

❑ Give yourself permission to be distracted. Sometimes, the best thing you can do is tune out what you're hearing and appreciate the beauty of the stained glass windows.

*The value of the Office is its objectivity. It is a means by which we pray with the whole church, uniting our prayer with that of millions of other Christians living and dead. This is true whether one is alone or in a group, for the Office is essentially a corporate act. It is objective too in that it does not depend on our feelings, but gives our prayer life a regularity and a disciplined framework.*

**Kenneth Leech,** *True Prayer*

# Three

## The Daily Practice

### The Daily Prayers of the Church—Daily Office

Ask a group of people, "For a Muslim, what is the expectation for daily prayer?" You are almost certain to get back a chorus of "Pray five times a day." Ask a group of Episcopalians what the Anglican tradition is and you will likely be met with blank stares.

Why don't we hear much about the details of "the tradition"? Part of the problem may be that we can feel uncomfortable talking about practices that arise from common use and long-term tradition because we worry that people will feel judged or put-upon. I wonder if another part of the problem is that we have very few models for equipping people for prayer life or helping either the parish or individual parishioners adapt the traditions in ways that make sense for them. We are simultaneously too rigid and too afraid of appearing rigid.

The norm for spiritual practice in the Anglican tradition (and central to the spiritual map we offer in this book) follows this pattern: Weekly Eucharist and daily corporate prayer (the Office).

The pattern in most real-life parishes is: Sunday Eucharist at 8 and 10; a mid-week Eucharist on Wednesdays; and, perhaps, general exhortation of the laity that they should pray more. The parish may or may not supplement these exhortations with a number of resources for personal prayer, such as journaling, centering prayer, or practices from other religious traditions. Accordingly, lay people looking for information and help on how to engage Anglican spiritual practices may find little available to them in the parish.

The Prayer Book itself devotes about two thirds of its pages to Eucharist, Office, and materials meant to support them. Yet many consider any attempt to engage the Daily Office *daily* as "too much," or "unrealistic." When Bob Gallagher and I taught a course in Anglican Spirituality at our parish, we mentioned the traditional pattern. One of the participants explained that she had an extensive daily meditation practice and that it was simply too much to be expected to add something else. I didn't argue with her about that, but I also didn't back away from the fact that this pattern *is* the tradition. More important, though, through the course we offered resources, methods, and approaches that permitted innovation and allowed participants to meaningfully engage the patterns of the wider church.

The parishioner with the meditation practice did not stop what she was doing but she did figure out methods to engage the prayers of the church in addition to what she was already doing. For her, this involved buying Daily Office books and using time spent commuting on the bus to say the Office. In subsequent conversations, she has talked about how important this has been for her and how it has deepened her experience of the Eucharist as well as her sense of connection to the parish and to the wider world.

Why is the daily practice important? Just as we need the weekly practice of Eucharist to renew our baptismal identity, we need a daily method of connecting to something bigger than ourselves. Again, just like with Eucharist, the daily prayers of the church are not *our* prayers. They are said in communion with Christians around the world and throughout time. They transcend our feelings and they transcend our loneliness, whether said alone or said with others present.

## Characteristics of the daily prayers of the church[4]

Central and intertwined characteristics include that they take place *daily*; that they are *corporate* in nature; and that they are both *structured* and *flexible* while "retaining a natural brevity that can be expanded if circumstances merit."

In the Office, we have an opportunity to re-connect each day with our identity as members of the Christian church while

---

[4] I am indebted for the structure and emphasis of this section and the next to S.F. Winward's essay entitled "The Daily Office," the introductory chapter of the Joint Liturgical Group's 1968 book of the same name.

focusing on the objective worship of God, rather than on our individual wants and needs.

Whether we are physically alone or with others, we participate in a cycle and a rhythm of prayer that includes the rest of the Church. And the Office, while flexible enough to adjust to our circumstances and individual time constraints (e.g., reading it on the bus, over the Internet, in the church, or with family and friends before dinner), nonetheless retains its own recognized integrity and content that has nothing to do with our feelings in the moment. These elements make the Office *corporate*, not personal.

The issue of objective, God-centered prayer versus individual, petition-based prayer deserves some fleshing out. Clearly we are expected to bring our own concerns to God, to pray that God's will for us and those we love will be fulfilled. And the Office does provide some space for personal petitions, but that space is not key to its structure.

Looking around at myself, my family and friends, the people I work with, and the broader culture, I don't sense that our problem is an inadequately-developed attention to self or to our own needs, desires and preferences. I do, though, think that we may have an inadequately-developed attention to the self that matures in an atmosphere of conscious focus on Christ and of wonder and awe in the presence of God and his kingdom. It is these elements of the self that are best nurtured by Eucharist and Office, and it is Reflection that helps us integrate and focus them, including in our personal prayer life.

The structure of the Office requires us to participate in something that is not of our own making. We say the Church's prayers, not our own. We read the assigned psalms, the assigned passages from the Bible, not the ones we are drawn to. The Office is not, though, onerous or resistant to adaptation and therefore exerts a gentle pressure on us.

It is a meaningful yet tolerable incursion into the world as we create it; and it is therefore a sometimes uncomfortable reminder that we are not the Creator and worship is not about us.

Another characteristic of the Office is that it is non-clerical and non-hierarchical. As a layperson who sometimes has authority issues (otherwise known as healthy skepticism, ahem), I greatly appreciate this aspect. The Prayer Book refers to the leader of the Office as the "Officiant," with no assumption that such person is a priest or other ordained person, and with no parts of the service reserved for the clergy. (Granted, if a Bishop is present, he or she gets to conclude the Office with a blessing, but I find that pastoral and unifying, as well as hierarchical.)

I am continually surprised by how rarely lay people are encouraged and assisted to embrace the one form of corporate worship that they can truly make their own and even routinely lead publicly without clergy in attendance.[5] From this standpoint, I think the Office is critical in countering the institutional church's tendency to over-direct and spoon-feed the laity while shying away from actually requiring anything of them.

When lay people start saying the Office it represents both the acceptance of a primary element of traditional Anglican spiritual life—and therefore an assent to the broader community—and a fundamental acceptance of personal responsibility for our own spiritual lives.

## What is the value of the church's daily prayer?

The daily nature of the church's prayers is a recognition of the human need for ongoing and regular nourishment, for regular grounding in the truth of the transcendent God and the mediation of the Incarnate Lord. We need to be part of something—and come up against something—bigger than we are, and we need to

---

[5] Some dioceses are increasing their control of this, imposing centralized licensing processes and requiring lengthy and often irrelevant "training" (theoretical and academic rather than practical and experiential) before the laity may offer the Office in the parish. I hope this does not become a trend and instead authority will be centered on parish clergy, who will work with parishioners to ensure they understand the structure of the Office and the liturgical norms of the particular parish, and to provide practical training, coaching, and oversight. Dioceses should encourage widespread lay participation in the Office, rather than discouraging it through excessive, even if well-meaning, bureaucracy.

do that frequently and independent of our transient feelings of holiness or happiness or heartbreak.

Martin Thornton describes the Office as the "prayer of Christ to the Father through the living members of the Body," and for me that description gets at the reality of daily prayer as at once the most mystical and the most mundane of endeavors.

We regular folks offer up our prayers, singly or in groups, relying on an ancient and established pattern. We do this knowing that it our responsibility to do so, that we offer our prayers for ourselves and on behalf of those members who are not able to join us. We also know that we are supported in our work by the prayers of other members of the Body. By our own act of daily will, we both expand upon and conform to the perpetually lively Body of Christ in a disciplined, intentional way.

> *I'm fed up with this ghastly picture of prayer as a private telephone line with or without a voice at the other end. It's much more like you and me playing our second fiddles in an unending heavenly orchestral symphony of praise and joy. When we pray, we take up our fiddles, and when we stop we put them down again—but the music never stops.* Basil Moss, quoted in *Spirituality for Today (London, 1967)*

## How does it work?

There are several ways to learn to say the Office. The first is to get a Prayer Book and a Bible, or the very snazzy Daily Office books that contain the liturgies and all the readings in one place.

An easier way (and certainly less expensive than the Daily Office books) is to log-on to websites that offer it. A good one is sponsored by Mission St. Clare and takes you through Morning and Evening Prayer, both Rite I and Rite II. It's simple to follow and gives you a good sense of the structure without the instructions and choices that make the Prayer Book Office look a little more complex than it is.

The Prayer Book itself includes liturgies for Morning Prayer and Evening Prayer (both Rite I and Rite II); a short Noonday Office; Compline; short devotions intended for family use, and a general Order for Evening. Morning Prayer and Evening Prayer are, however, the heart of the Office and they're the best place to start to get a sense of the structure and content.

The basic structure of the Office is simple: Assigned psalm, assigned scripture reading, and the prayers of the Church. The assigned psalms and Bible readings appear in the back of the Prayer Book, in the section titled Daily Lectionary (we'll come back to this). If you read through the liturgies, however, you see that there are other elements, such as hymns, canticles, confession, and the Apostles Creed. The "prayers of the Church" can be relatively brief or relatively long, and include the Lord's Prayer, numerous Collects, prayers for mission, and standardized intercessory prayers called suffrages.

The order of service and the various options for public worship are laid out in the italicized rubrics, or instructions, that accompany the text of the services. Obviously, you have some more choices when you're saying it privately than when you're leading the Office at the parish. In either event, though, there are choices to be made that affect the length, content, and rhythm of the Office.

## Prayer Book Daily Lectionary

Returning to the Daily Lectionary at the back of the Prayer Book, the Lectionary is divided into two sections that appear on facing pages—Year One and Year Two. The Lectionary follows the church year and therefore begins in Advent, not in January. Year One begins on the First Sunday of Advent preceding odd-numbered years, and Year Two begins on the First Sunday of Advent preceding even-numbered years.

Simply turn to the *Daily* Lectionary (not the plain old Lectionary, which lays out the readings for Sunday Eucharist in churches that aren't using the Revised Common Lectionary), make the calculation that allows you to determine whether you're in Year One or Year Two, and then flip through the pages till you find the right date based on the season.

Note that the Season After Pentecost is identified by dates closest to a particular Sunday and the assigned readings and collects appear under headings with numbered "Propers" close to a particular Sunday. So if you start saying the Office during Ordinary Time, say in September, you'll just have to poke around a bit until you find the closest date.

Detailed instructions appear at the beginning of the Daily Lectionary. In general, be aware that the numbers listed by themselves represent psalms. They are separated by a stylized asterisk—the psalm or psalms before the asterisk are usually said at Morning Prayer, while the psalm or psalms after the asterisk are usually said at Evening Prayer. When saying the Office on your own, you can pick one or more.

There will also be three Bible readings assigned—one from the Hebrew Scriptures, an Epistle, and a Gospel reading. Again, you can select one or more readings if you are saying it on your own. The Daily Lectionary covers the majority of the Bible in a two-year period.

## A note on canticles

The instructions for both Morning and Evening Prayer say that a Canticle should be sung or said after each Lesson. Canticles are non-metrical hymns taken from Biblical sources other than the

Psalms. The Morning Prayer service provides 14 different canticles within the text. Evening Prayer provides the traditional ones for the evening—the Song of Mary (the *Magnificat*) and the Song of Simeon (the *Nunc Dimittas*)—within the text and permits the use of any from Morning Prayer. The traditional canticle for Morning Prayer is Canticle 4 or 16 (Rite I or Rite II), the Song of Zechariah.

My first experience of the Office was with Evening Prayer, but I had snuck a look at Morning Prayer. I vowed never to say it because I feared I would be forced to run through all of those canticles. Upon further inspection, however, I realized that they were simply options and that, although they are the traditional canticles, I was not even wedded to the *Magnificat* or *Nunc Dimittas* at Evening Prayer. Since then, I mostly stick to the time-honored but sometimes I also enjoy thinking ahead and selecting canticles appropriate to the season and the lessons.

**WAYS TO ENGAGE THE OFFICE**

❑ Experiment and be flexible! Keep this mantra in mind while reading the rest of these suggestions.

❑ Use different methods that work for you. For example, many have begun to use Internet resources, which lay out all readings and prayers for the day. My own practice is to say the Morning Office after I arrive at work and get my coffee, but before I start reading e-mail. For others, holding the Prayer Book and the Bible is an important part of the ritual. Daily Office books, while pricey, have been invaluable for some because they contain all needed information in one compact volume.

❑ Focus on a time of day when you won't feel immediately burdened and when you can rely on regularly having 10-20 minutes available to you. For some people, the morning works best; for others, they can reliably say the Office at the dinner table; and others find Compline in bed is the ticket.

❑ Start small and avoid taking on too much. For instance, don't decide that you will go from saying no Office to saying Morning Prayer, Noonday Prayer, Evening Prayer and Compline. The likelihood of this sort of radical change working is small and the result is that you may well end up disheartened and not doing anything.

❑ Try a particular time or way of saying the Office for a week and then reflect on how it's working for you. Were you able to do what you set out to do? What worked? What didn't work? Consider whether there are alterations you could make and try for another week. Reflect again and adjust as needed.

❑ Recruit others to help you. Even if you can't physically be together, it can be useful to agree with a friend or family member that you will say the Office at the same time.

❑ Consider ways to involve your children. Learning how to look up the readings or psalms and lead the service can actually be fun. The simplified "Devotions for Families" could be usefully adapted as part of mealtimes or as a bedtime ritual.

❑   When saying the Office alone, remember that you are part of the Body of Christ and that you are saying it corporately even though no one else is present. Use the words "we," "us," and "our" and know that you offer up the prayers of the Church on behalf of yourself and others.

❑   Commit to saying the Office but be willing to adapt when needed without beating yourself up over it. Maybe you usually do two Bible readings but today you can only manage one. It might be that you regularly focus on the most basic structure: psalm, scripture, the church's prayers, and leave out the canticles, confession, and Creed. On some days the most you may able to do is to say the Lord's Prayer or a fragment of a psalm. That is still participating in the daily prayers of the Church.

❑   If you are part of a parish that says the Office communally, try to attend once a week, maybe on the same day each week.

❑   Think of the Office as part of a system of prayer—the other elements are weekly Eucharist and Reflection, which may include personal prayer. Eucharist and Office form the ground out of which your personal prayer—which is truly individualistic and fed by your personality—is based. Strengthening one element strengthens the others.

❑   Talk to others in your parish (including the clergy!) to see if it might be feasible to develop teams of parish-trained laypeople who could regularly lead the Office. Working together makes saying the Office easier and even a small cadre of parishioners regularly saying the Office together will effect a change in the parish's community life and in the parish's experience of the Eucharist.

❑   If you are saying the Office at your parish, consider working with parish clergy to develop a simple reference card that lays out the basics of the service. The card could describe the practices in your parish (e.g., how the psalm is read; if a particular canticle is used on certain days, etc.), and which elements are typically included. This is helpful for those attending services at the church, in that everyone knows what's expected, there is some order and rhythm, and it minimizes the need for disruptive announcements ("Please turn to such-and-such a page." "We will say the psalm antiphonally, beginning on the side of the Officiant." "We will say the *Magnificat* after the Gospel reading.")

## AREAS FOR REFLECTION

☐ Are there elements of the Office that are particularly difficult for you? What are they? Notice what, if anything, is hard for you and consider whether this comes up in other areas of your life, including your spiritual life.

☐ What is it like to say the Office when you don't want to? What feelings or thoughts come up for you? How do they change after you've said the Office?

☐ How does saying the Office connect you to the broader Christian community?

☐ What impact does saying the Office daily have on your daily life?

☐ What impact does saying the Office have on your experience of Eucharist? On your own ability to reflect?

## Assessing Your Use of the Daily Office

**1. In experimenting with the Daily Office this past week:**

| What I found most helpful, might have reinforced saying the Office | What I found most difficult or challenging |
| --- | --- |
| | |

**2. All prayer must be chosen and owned. Our ability to sustain a practice is dependent on:**

**a. Having adequate and useful information**

In regard to the Office this is likely to include having experimented with several ways of saying the Office to find one that fits for now.

| I have enough information to have adequately experimented | | | | I need to gather a lot more information and experiment more |
| --- | --- | --- | --- | --- |
| 1 | 2 | 3 | 4 | 5 |

## b. Free choice

Making use of the Office needs to come from free choice rather than being stuck in our habits, internal "shoulds" or external pressure from others. Free choice depends on having enough information, including experimentation.

| I feel pressure to do the Office— from others, as a "should" within myself | | | | My pattern of saying the Office is grounded in reasons that make a lot of sense to me and offers rewards I desire. |
|---|---|---|---|---|
| 1 | 2 | 3 | 4 | 5 |

## c. Internal commitment

Shows itself in being sustainable; not much internal resistance. Internal commitment depends on the extent of free choice you have.

| Doesn't seem sustainable for me at this time in my life' too much internal resistance in me | | | | I feel very much at peach with saying the Daily Office; this seems sustainable. |
|---|---|---|---|---|
| 1 | 2 | 3 | 4 | 5 |

**3. Your connection with the spiritual rationale of the Office.**

*Which of these attract you, speak to you?*

\_\_\_\_    *enters the ancient cycle of prayer* Evelyn Underhill,

\_\_\_\_    *a means by which we pray with the whole church, uniting our prayer with that of millions of other Christians living and dead.* Kenneth Leech

\_\_\_\_    *we became more and more aware of the living reality of the invisible "communion of saints* Jonathan Daniels

\_\_\_\_    *It feeds into the invisible economy of Grace, God's hidden plumbing, for the good of the world keep ourselves in constant awareness of the divine order; an order of love and justice which embraces and underlies all order* Father George Guiver CR

\_\_\_\_    *The most important thing the Office does for me is to pry me out of my own agenda, not by helping me ignore my feelings, whatever they might be, but by giving me a place to put them.* Bryan Carr

\_\_\_\_    *I come to the text where I am at, and just by virtue of engaging with it (reading it), the Spirit works, often invisibly, sometimes visibly.* Susan Forshey

**4. Which need does the Office primarily address for you?**
(Either orientation is legitimate; at times we need one more than the other)

\_\_\_\_    For prayer as comfort; needs to touch my emotions; needs to feel gentle and encouraging

\_\_\_\_    For prayer as discipline; a form of self-giving; of loving obedience. (Father George Guiver CR)

# Daily Office—Short Forms

A way of participating in the Daily Office is to use a form you have memorized. For it to be the Office and not your Personal Devotions the form needs to be the "prayers of the church."

### A Morning Office—Inclusive Language

Psalm:

O God, you are my God; from the break of day I seek you.   Psalm 63

Reading:

Beloved, since God loved us so much, we ought to love one another. For if we love one another, God abides in us, and God's love will be perfected in us.  I John 4

The Prayers
Offer Intercessions and Thanksgivings

Sun of Righteousness, so gloriously risen, shine in our hearts as we celebrate our redemption.

### End of Day Office—Inclusive Language

Psalm:
Yours is the day, O God, yours also the night; you established the moon and the sun.  Psalm 141

Reading:

You have come to the help of your servant Israel, and you have remembered your promise of mercy.  Luke 1: 54

The Prayers
Offer Intercessions and Thanksgivings

Send forth upon us the Spirit of love, that in companionship with one another your abounding grace may increase among us; through Jesus Christ. Amen

# Daily Office—Short Forms

### A Morning Office

Psalm:

For the Lord is good; his mercy is everlasting; and his faithfulness endures from age to age. Psalm 100

Reading:

In the tender compassion of our God the dawn from on high shall break upon us, to shine on those who dwell in darkness and the shadow of death, and to guide our feet into the way of peace - Luke 1:78 - 79

The Prayers
Offer Intercessions and Thanksgivings

In you we live and move and have our being. Amen


### End of Day Office

Psalm:

Behold now, bless the Lord, all you servants of the Lord, you that stand by night in the house of the Lord. * Lift up your hands in the holy place and bless the Lord; the Lord who made heaven and earth bless you out of Zion.  Psalm 134

Reading:
Lord, you now have set your servant free
   to go in peace as you have promised;
For these eyes of mine have seen the Savior,
   Whom you have prepared for all the world to see:
A light to enlighten the nations,
   And the glory of your people Israel.  Luke 2:29 - 32

The Prayers
Offer Intercessions and Thanksgivings

Guide us waking, O Lord, and guard us sleeping; that awake we may watch with Christ, and asleep we may rest in peace.

*There is a silent self within us whose presence is disturbing precisely because it is so silent: it can't be spoken. It has to remain silent. To articulate it, to verbalize it, is to tamper with it, and in some ways to destroy it.*

**Thomas Merton: Essential Writings**

# Four

# Reflection

As the collect has it, "we are placed among things which are passing away," and we are "to hold fast to those that shall endure." Sorting one from the other is the work of Reflection.

If Weekly Eucharist and Daily Prayers of the Church are the ground of spiritual life, then Reflection grows in that soil. It develops in response to corporate worship and is shaped in accordance with the personality, preferences and gifts of the individual. Reflection is a focused lens through which the individual considers his or her life as formed by the worship and doctrine of the Christian faith.

Reflection contains our own ways of connecting with God in a manner that suits us and that allows us to engage in petition, self-examination and confession, intercession, thanksgiving, and adoration. Reflection aids our ability to be grounded and centered. It helps us connect daily life to God. And it is a critical part of how we consider the extent and impact of our own sinfulness—the specific and idiosyncratic ways in which we try to distance ourselves from the love of God.

In the spiritual practices map we have described, individual Reflection is clearly informed by Eucharist and the Daily prayers, but is itself based on our personalities and definitely about our own preferences and style. How does each of us, as a unique child of God, best approach the mind of God and respond to his call to us?

## Forms of Reflection

I have led brainstorming exercises with lay people in which they list the various forms of prayer or means of disciplined reflection they have used in their lives. They then follow up with the forms that have been most helpful to them and that they have been able to sustain over time. Examples include, in no particular order:

- ➤ Saying the rosary
- ➤ Talking with friends
- ➤ Walking a labyrinth
- ➤ Centering prayer
- ➤ Spiritual direction
- ➤ Walking
- ➤ Meditation
- ➤ Spontaneous thanksgiving
- ➤ Grace at meals
- ➤ Personal rituals
- ➤ AA meetings
- ➤ Therapy
- ➤ Journaling
- ➤ Silent retreats

While this list is by no means exhaustive, it does illustrate the wide range of ways in which people are able to consider the circumstances of their lives and enter into deeper relationship with God.

## Space and time—engaging silence, engaging connection

The quote from Marva Dawn that began the section on silence in Eucharist is equally appropriate here.

> It is impossible for our inner selves to be prepared to be open to God and receptive to God's Word until we silence our sinful selves—our efforts to be in control, to manipulate everything and everyone to accomplish our own purposes....We need the channel of silence to transport us from the busy harbors of our tensions out to the ocean of God's infinite being. *Reaching Out Without Dumbing Down*

A critical element in becoming more reflective is creating space for it.  Making time, cutting out extraneous activity, developing a capacity for silence and stillness.  Sometimes, we can make space or create silence by what we *don't* do: ride the bus to work without listening to an iPod, checking email, or reading a book; put the book down before you're tired enough to fall asleep; turn off the TV when you're not watching it; drive without music or news.

None of these things is bad, but occasionally *not* doing them may help bring our awareness to the emptiness of silence, the darkness of what we may obscure through doing, noise, and entertainment.  And in that emptiness and darkness we can become better known to ourselves and better able to see where God is already present to us and where he is looking to fill and illuminate our lives.

In *Girl Meets God,* Lauren Winner describes one Lent in which she gave up reading.  It is a marvelous example of how something virtuous, when taken to excess, can become a vehicle for sin.  I followed Ms. Winner's example myself for a couple of years running and was startled by how easily I used books to avoid responsibility, engagement, and the sheer terror of confronting the silence of simply being in the presence of God.

I still love to read and it remains my preferred form of recreation, but six years after my experiment with *not* reading as a religious discipline, I find that I can go to sleep without a book, I pay more attention to the people and needs in front of me, and I am more faithful in prayer and worship.  I can't guarantee that there's a direct relationship, but there is definitely a connection between my directly addressing a form of compulsive avoidance expressed as compulsive activity, and a growing spiritual maturity.

Related to developing a capacity for silence and stillness is developing the capacity to really see and hear other people, and to connect with them without losing ourselves.  Technology has made it much easier to move through life without noticing what or who is around us, and in some cases to avoid actual engagement with others.  Email, for example, permits us to deliver difficult messages without having to see the expression on the other person's face.  Similarly, when we get a message we don't want to read, we can press the delete key.

One obvious dynamic of modern life is ever-present music over earphones, as well as ever-present cell phone conversations, whether our own or those of others. Again, while neither listening to music nor talking on the phone is inherently wrong, the constant presence of these activities allows us to maintain the illusion that we operate in a protected bubble of our own making.

In some ways, earphones provide an excuse to avoid common courtesy—we literally don't hear what people ask us or notice the response of those around us. Ignoring other people thereby becomes somehow acceptable, even though we choose to create the circumstances that make listening impossible. It also inures us to our impact on others—if we're all in a bubble, what difference does my bubble make? We'll just bounce harmlessly off one another.

Within this context, it's important to remember that Christian denominations, and even different congregations within the same denomination, differ widely in their view of the importance of silence and a sense of sacred "time apart" in worship. Where we do not have much opportunity during communal worship to make this space, it is particularly important to do so in a disciplined way in our personal lives.

Darkness, death, and sin are present for all of us and we have little support from the broader culture to deal with those areas in a way that enables us to grapple productively with the reality of our own decisions, the impact of our own blindness, and the consequences of our own sins. It is certainly common to feel guilty or inadequate, but it is quite another matter to connect our failings, our shadows, to those virtues and gifts of the spirit that represent wholeness in Christ.

In other words, we must have the discipline and courage to confront the shadows while also developing ways to recognize and deepen the manifestations around us of our own joy, love and service.

## What are Christians called to be?

When considering what kind of person, what kind of Christian, we are called to become—and therefore the shape our reflection will take—it is helpful to have concrete ideas in mind of what that looks like from several different perspectives. It is also helpful to have concrete descriptions of both sin and Christian virtue. The following is excerpted with permission from *Fill All Things: The Dynamics of Spirituality in the Parish Church*, © Robert Gallagher 2008.

### One Baptized into the Body of Christ

A new person in Christ; becoming salt, light and leaven; growing up in Christ. " [B]uried with Christ in his death...share in his resurrection...reborn by the Holy Spirit." ..."[A]n inquiring and discerning heart, the courage to will and to persevere, a spirit to know and to love you, and the gift of joy and wonder in all your works." A believer in God—Father, Son and Holy Spirit; called to "persevere in resisting evil, and, whenever you fall into sin, repent and return...proclaim by word and example the Good News...seek and serve Christ in all persons...strive for justice and peace among all people, and respect the dignity of every human being." (From *The Book of Common Prayer*, Baptism liturgy.)

### The Full Stature of Christ

There is, of course, Paul's understanding of what God is doing in our lives, e.g. in Ephesians that we are to grow into the full stature of Christ; that the graces and practices necessary for that growth are humility, gentleness, patience, forbearance born of love, eagerness to maintain unity in the bond of peace, truthfulness mediated in love, mutual kindness, tenderheartedness and forgiveness; and in Galatians that the fruit of the spirit is love, joy, peace, patience, kindness, generosity, faithfulness, gentleness and self-control.

### Seven Gifts of the Holy Spirit

**Fear (awe)**. ...[F]ear that you will not have the life you could have; the life God wants for you. It is as opposed to a life that is not for "the good" or that is trivial. This is the "fear that establishes proportions and recognizes consequences" and may lead "to a realistic, rueful … almost humorous awareness of our true state."[6]

**Piety (affection).** A kind of fondness or love, a recognition of what you "owe the land that bred you," gratitude for the love, forgiveness and understanding one receives.

**Knowledge.** A capacity to accept paradox, to hold things in balance, to see more completely. It is the knowledge of God and the dynamics of awe and affection.

**Courage (fortitude).** Closing the gap between belief and action "by reaching beyond themselves to Christ," rather than "by pulling Christ towards them and adapting him to their own uses." Standing fast even though you want to run. Especially needed in moral life, the world of ideas, and in personal relations.

**Counsel (guidance).** An openness to the Holy Spirit; openness to an energy for good that comes from beyond ourselves. It is related to developing a capacity for listening and an inner silence.

**Understanding.** The gift of balance, an awareness of the situation. It is "knowing when to celebrate and when to lament." This is self knowledge. It is seeing the world rightly—that the creation is good, that God is encountered through it.

**Wisdom.** The coming together of the other six gifts; wholeness.

### Seven Deadly Sins

A definition of sin offered by Richard Holloway (one-time presiding bishop of Scotland) is "a wrongly directed effort; a good drive that fails to find the right object; a good thing in itself that is done to excess." (*Seven to Flee, Seven to Follow,* 1986.) This fits Newman's understanding that, "Evil has no substance of its own,

---

[6] Martin Thornton, in *The Rock and the River,* describes Holy Fear as "the joyous expression of an habitual recognition of divine transcendence which bubbles over into life as that exciting awe and reverence so aptly described…as 'numinous'.…It is that exhilarating, terrifying, dynamic insight into the glory and majesty of God which inspires a sense of wonder in all creation together with a calm recollection and faith in Providence."

but is only the defect, excess, perversion, or corruption of that which has substance."

Martin Smith, in his book on reconciliation, urges, "Fix your mind on the positive virtues, of which sins are the shadow." In a related understanding, Martin Thornton viewed the purpose of self-examination as aiming at *"tranquillitas*; not the suppression of desire, not *apatheia*, but harmony between the elements of personality." So, in all this we are dealing with health and wholeness rather than simply avoidance and self-protection.

In some of the material below [Robert Gallagher is] drawing on Holloway's work.

**Pride.** Self esteem raised to an inordinate level, so that all sense of proportion is lost.

**Envy (jealousy).** "Sorrow for another's good," "Satisfaction at the misfortunes of our friends." A characteristic of envy is that it offers no real pleasure, it is without fun; other sins offer some gratification. Symptoms include malice, being good at noticing the defects in others, hypocrisy, dejection. Envy may lead into the third sin.

**Covetousness (avarice).** "Itching hunger for the good things of life" (success, possessions, popularity). It shows itself in conspicuous consumption of things or people, fear of aging. [Note: pride and envy are rooted in a sense of inadequacy. There is in us a "deep longing to be accepted and appreciated; the need is to know that we are loved as we are."]

**Anger.** A disproportionate response to danger; phases that are destructive—impatience, retaliation, lack of control, resentment. The antidotes are to give ourselves to systematically willing another person's good and to act quickly as anger breaks out to minimize the damage.

**Lust.** A distorted instinct that is good in itself. It is rooted in a pursuit of pleasure that gives permission for exploitation, even if mutually agreed upon. There is a danger of moving into an addictive cycle and diminishing one's capacity for committed, joyful relationships. C.S. Lewis saw this as the least significant of the sins.

**Gluttony.** Much the same as the above in its dynamics. The person is driven to a pursuit of satisfying appetites—too much drink, food, smoking, talk; compulsive behavior. They are natural instincts that are allowed to play a disproportionate role and can end up dominating the personality. An approach to lust and gluttony is learning self discipline and to redirect the instincts toward "the good."

**Sloth.** "The instinct for rest and creative idling taken and distorted into an unattractive passivity," "everything is too much trouble." It is a disease of the will, it numbs the will. Instead of taking our life in our own hand we drift along, not really being bad people (we don't have the energy for it). Sloth does create the conditions under which evil takes hold in society. It may be related to why people seem to resist "giving themselves" to another, to their work, and to civic life.

## *Four Cardinal Virtues*

The four are interdependent; if you don't adequately possess one of them, the others are distorted in some fashion.

**Prudence.** In the most down-to-earth meaning we are speaking of having good sense; the capacity for practical judgment. The virtue of it is in being grounded in reality and directed toward what is good. It assumes openness to reality. This is not the same thing as excess caution and a withholding spirit.

**Justice.** The virtue is rooted in the assumption that we live with one another. That then presents us with several issues to address, including what we as individuals owe society; what we owe other individuals; and what society owes individuals.

**Fortitude.** This is about removing barriers to justice. A central element is perseverance. Justice is only possible when we stay with the work before us. It is not the same as stubbornness.

**Temperance.** Self-awareness and self-control are needed if we are to enjoy life and at the same time be good people. The work that has been done in recent decades on emotional and social intelligence is a resource.

## AREAS FOR REFLECTION

❏ Look at the list of reflective practices provided earlier in this chapter, and add any you've used. Pick one or two that you can begin using. Try for a month and reflect on how it went. What did you learn? What did you notice? What would you like to continue? Do more of? Is there something else you'd like to try?

❏ Consider elements of your own personality. Are you introverted or extraverted? Are you more drawn to religious symbol and metaphor or disciplined analysis of theological concepts? Which forms of Reflection would be most likely to support and nurture your existing personality and preferences? Which might stretch you some but still be supportive of what is? Which seem counter-productive for you?

❏ Experiment with silence and stillness. Try being at home without the TV, radio, or other music on. Avoid video games or the Internet for a specified period of time each day. Whatever you choose *not* to do, replace the lack of activity with intentional stillness (physical silence) and with silence. How did you feel? What did you notice? What feelings—both physical and emotional—came up for you?

❏ Experiment with engagement. Talk to your partner or spouse, another family member, or a close friend for a few minutes each day for a month at the same time (e.g., dinnertime or before going to bed). Agree on a structure and content you would both find helpful. Examples are, talking about something you did that day, something that is worrying you, something that you're happy about. Agree to listen to the other person with attentiveness— don't multi-task—and in a supportive and non-judgmental way. Aim to really understand the other person. Ask clarifying questions, if needed, but don't give advice. Switch roles. How did that feel? How did your reactions, thoughts, and feelings differ when you were the person listening versus the person talking? What behaviors in yourself help you feel connected? Distant? How did it feel to switch the roles? Is one more comfortable than the other?

❑ Read through the list of Four Cardinal Virtues. What strikes you? What feelings and thoughts are you aware of? Are you particularly drawn to one of the virtues? Particularly repelled by one of them?

❑ Again considering the Four Cardinal Virtues, what do you make of the statement, "The four are interdependent; if you don't adequately possess one of them, the others are distorted in some fashion." How do you notice that playing out in your own life?

❑ Read through the Seven Gifts of the Spirit and the Seven Deadly Sins. Can you see a connection in your own life to the Sins as shadows of the Gifts? What do you make of Newman's quote? "Evil has no substance of its own, but is only the defect, excess, perversion, or corruption of that which has substance."

*We are one, after all, you and I. Together we suffer,
together exist, and forever will recreate each other.*

**Pierre Teilhard de Chardin**

*In our world full of strangers, estranged from their own
past, culture and country, from their neighbors, friends and
family, from their deepest self and their God, we witness a
painful search for a hospitable place where life can be
lived without fear and where community can be
found...[T]hat is our vocation: to convert the* hostis *into a*
hospes, *the enemy into a guest and to create the free and
fearless space where brotherhood and sisterhood can be
formed and fully experienced.*

**Henri Nouwen, *Reaching Out***

# Five

# Participating in Community

## Defining the community we seek

A frequently-cited reason for joining a church is the desire to be part of a community. The term is bandied about in many areas of parish life, but it is seldom that we come together to define the sort of community we seek or to reflect on how we might best shape it. We may also find it difficult to see that our participation in the community is itself a spiritual practice and a spiritual discipline. I know that I have, more often than I care to admit, seen the community as a place to get my needs met, and where I can come and go as the fancy strikes me.

I have sometimes heard descriptions of church life that contain a significant undercurrent of utopian assumption: that somehow "Christian community" necessarily involves a lot of altruism, kindness, and an unfailing ability to detect and deliver what each person needs to feel included and loved. Of course, I have sometimes heard the bitter recrimination and cries of "hypocrites!" that follow the inevitable discovery that these vaguely articulated assumptions don't match the reality.

Creating "free and fearless space where brotherhood and sisterhood can be formed and fully experienced" won't happen without the mysterious and surprising interventions of the Holy Spirit. But it also won't happen without real work and intentional focus by the members of the community.

That a church community exists to worship God makes it fundamentally different from other groups, including social service organizations. The church is "not primarily for ourselves but for God." As Nouwen puts it, "the Christian community is not a closed circle of people embracing each other, but a forward-moving group of companions bound together by the same voice asking for their attention." If we consciously adopt that as our stance and see part of our purpose as attending to the call of that voice in community, it is less likely that the parish will become simply another demand on our time, or a place characterized by turf struggles and pet projects (however worthy).

To this end, I will talk in this chapter about "primary task." What is the main thing the parish community is trying to accomplish? There are a number of ways to think about this, but the one I find most helpful is that the parish needs to be focused on forming mature Christians. Formation occurs by nurturing the renewal of baptismal identity and purpose—who we are as baptized members of the body of Christ—and also nurturing apostolic living in daily life.

The parish church at its best fosters a healthy movement between renewal and action, between identity and behavior, between conscious reliance on God and sub-conscious reliance on God as the ground of all we do.

"Renewal" occurs in worship, study, the parish's social life, and being equipped for Christian action. Our "Apostolate" is our participation in the work of Christ in service, evangelization and stewardship in the areas of workplace, family and friends, civic life, and the church.[7]

While both the business world and many non-profits have spent considerable time, money, and energy ensuring that their vision, mission, and core values are aligned and consistent with their daily practices and that the organization's sense of primary task is widely understood throughout the organization, the church may have been less successful with this.

If we come to understand that the Church has a specific task—and that its task is not that of any other organization—it becomes easier to take steps to create communities that will help members grow into mature Christians. When each one of has an idiosyncratic, and often unarticulated, view of the primary task of church it is almost certain that we will fail in creating the community we need as we fumble around trying to create the community we think we want.

---

[7] From Robert Gallagher's Renewal—Apostolate Cycle. © 2008, all rights reserved. Used with permission.

## The dynamics of human gathering

While it is critical to understand the theological and mystical qualities of the parish church, it is also critical to recognize what people actually tend to do when they come together. Groups develop, evolve, stagnate and disintegrate in many predictable patterns. Those processes can be addressed in ways that result in better functioning and that channel destructive tendencies into new life.

M. Scott Peck, in his 1987 book *The Different Drum: Community Making and Peace*, asserts that most communities are dysfunctional in varying degrees due to an inability to create true communal cooperation within their group. Instead of cooperation, there is conflict—both obvious and subtle—and the aims of the community are therefore much more difficult to realize. Peck classifies the process of moving from dysfunctional to functional community in four stages: Pseudo Community, Chaos, Emptiness, and True Community.

**Pseudo Community** exists where the group pretends everything is fine, even though it is not. The group claims that everyone is in agreement, everyone is happy with the status quo, and any problems that emerge are glossed over. Since no one will admit to existing problems, they are never addressed, and the organization is an inefficient body guided by mistrust, complicated work-arounds, and apathy. It is not a happy place, but dissatis-factions are only aired in the parking lot, where they cannot be solved.

**Chaos** results where an individual finally admits to the group that there are problems, refuses to go along with the silence of the status quo, points a finger, or raises an uncomfortable question. Since the group has no coping skills, it descends into Chaos. It this situation, groups choose to either revert to Pseudo Community, or move to the next developmental step, Emptiness.

**Emptiness** is a time-out. It is defined more by what it is not than by what it is. The group refuses to cooperate or move on. But it does do some work. It is a time for reflection, fact checking, research, to "seek to understand rather than to be understood." This meditative, contemplative period can return to Chaos, or spontaneously move into the fourth stage, True Community.

**True Community** is the stage where the group flourishes. There is honest communication. Participants lose their mask of composure. People start to enjoy being with one another.

These descriptions are similar to a number of theories of group development and functioning. What I find particularly useful in this is the language—the use of the term "community" underscores that these same dynamics are present wherever human beings gather, even if the ostensible purpose is noble and intended to transcend the petty foibles we have to deal with in our regular life.

I have used this model in work with several parishes. One exercise is to have the members of the parish physically place themselves in various areas of the room that have been designated as corresponding to one of the four quadrants of community. The instruction is to place themselves where they see the parish now. The participants then talk together about what they make of that, why they positioned themselves where they did, what behaviors they see that led them to conclude the parish was in a particular place.

This is a useful way of getting people to talk about what community means, what they value, and how the existing parish both conforms to the members' images of community and the ways it doesn't.

## Communication skills

There are many models and approaches for dealing with more effective communication. One very simple model I've found useful was developed by James Ware, of Focus Consulting Group, a respected consultant to financial services companies. I have adapted the model for church use and am using it here with permission.

The model begins with the assumption that communication is foundational to culture, and that the ways we communicate are inextricably linked with the environment we create. Different patterns of communication, coupled with different skill levels, are connected to predictable, identifiable patterns of culture. This has important consequences for what our parish communities are like.

The model posits that the highest levels of communication must be grounded in a Relationship Orientation. From there, quality of communication is a function of the degree of Openness and Candor[8]. A diagram of the model appears after this section.

### Relationship Orientation

Characterized by an empathic stance—approachable, non-judgmental, curious, interested in the experiences and feelings of others, as well as the impact of your own behavior on others. Demonstrate integrity in interactions and broader areas of life. "People with a relatively disciplined, mature, full spiritual life; flexibility with self and others; an experimental and exploratory stance." (Robert Gallagher, *Fill All Things: The Spiritual Dynamics of the Parish Church*).

### Openness

Openness is the *receiving* half of any communication, listening. Involves learning to seek and listen to feedback. Focused on genuine understanding of the other person. Requires suspending your own beliefs, judgments, and need to be "right" and focusing attention on the speaker to improve your understanding. Active listening.

### Candor

Candor is the *sending* half of any communication. Being willing to tell the whole truth, without withholding. Being willing to share your feelings and experiences in the present moment, while taking responsibility for those feelings and experiences being your own. Recognizing the value in your view—and being willing to share it, advocate for it, and influence the system—while accepting that you don't possess the entire picture and that there are other valid perspectives and possibilities.

---

[8] In writing this, I have adapted and expanded on a description of James Ware's model in a paper by Jamie Goodrich Ziegler called "The 'Same-Page' Challenge," © 2008 Focus Consulting Group.

- **Relationship orientation.** Characterized by an empathic stance—approachable, non-judgmental, curious, interested in the experiences and feelings of others, as well as the impact of your own behavior on others. Demonstrate integrity in interactions and broader areas of life. "People with a relatively disciplined, mature, full spiritual life; flexibility with self and others; an experimental and exploratory stance."

- **Openness.** Openness is the *receiving* half of any communication, listening. Involves learning to seek and listen to feedback. Focused on genuine understanding of the other person. Requires suspending your own beliefs, judgments, and need to be "right" and focusing attention on the speaker to improve your understanding. Active listening.

- **Candor.** Candor is the *sending* half of any communication. Being willing to tell the whole truth, without withholding. Being willing to share your feelings and experiences in the present moment, while taking responsibility for those feelings and experiences being your own. Recognizing the value in your view—and being willing to share it, advocate for it, and influence the system—while accepting that you don't possess the entire picture and that there are other valid perspectives and possibilities.

**Collaborative Culture:** Highest levels of candor and openness. High trust, low turnover, easy to attract parishioners and staff. Clear about what we are and what we aren't—good cultural fit, high energy & creativity, win/win mindset, lower than average stress levels. Primary task = formation of Christians, renewal of baptismal identity.

**Competitive Culture.** Candor & openness both present, but not fully developed or practiced. Discussions debate-oriented—candor & openness not at highest levels: candor not open & revealing, openness not with intent to learn. Primary task = determining Truth.

**Careful Culture.** Listen to other views politely, but not willing to share their own opinions, don't address true issues. Gossip, anxiety about other's reactions, bureaucratic, turf-based & slow-moving. May be high loyalty, but limited creativity and low energy. Primary task = create sense of comfort and belonging.

**Aggressive Culture.** Willing to send message out but not to really listen. Say it louder and more forcefully if not being heard. Win/lose mentality. Blame. Schism. Primary task = imposing the right agenda/stance/doctrine.

**Fear-Based Culture.** "Victim" mentality, helpless, unable to speak up for what they want, cynical, closed to new ideas. Passive-aggressive. Gossip, defensiveness, blame. Lowest levels of trust. Primary task = providing structure, setting the rules, establishing consequences from outside & above.

Higher

C
A
N
D
O
R

Lower

OPENNESS

Higher

# Communication Models—Examples of Different Cultures

**Examples of Collaborative Culture:** Parish is an exciting, dynamic place to be. Parishioners are clear about baptismal identity and live into their apostolate at work, with friends and family, in the broader community, and at church. Things are happening based on organic energy and appropriate institutional support (little evidence of "we're doing this because we think we're supposed to" or begging for resources). Leaders and parishioners widely understand the primary task to be the formation of Christians and the renewal of baptismal identity. There is a strategic orientation—action takes place based on conscious attention to primary task. Leaders and Parishioners are willing to identify and discuss parish initiatives, worship elements, or forms of decision making that appear to run counter to furtherance of the primary task.

**Examples of Competitive Culture:** Candor and openness present but not fully mastered. There may be a debate rather than a listening orientation. The tone of discussions in the parish is more competitive—candor and openness are not at the highest levels, meaning that candor is not necessarily open and revealing, and openness may occur but without the intent to learn. This is probably the culture least likely to be sustained over time in the Episcopal Church, because of the relatively dominant tendency to tolerate ambiguity and value open-ended questions. Denominations that place a more pronounced value on the intellectual aspects of worship and on the propositional elements of faith may well be more at ease in a Competitive Culture. Episcopal parishes may be more likely to be stuck in Receptive or Aggressive Cultures with "Competitive" perhaps likely to be more of a transitional culture. The distortion of primary task may be seen in a focus on determining The Truth rather than on listening. There may be limited tolerance for accepting other parishioners at different places on their own spiritual journey. Methods for change: Focus on spiritual practice, emphasis on primary task, skill building, Benedictine practices around listening, stability, and conversions of life.

**Examples of Aggressive Culture:** In-fighting—difficult to implement change because there are entrenched "sides" to many issues. May have history of significant conflict with priests, high turnover. May be dominant groups who appear to dictate how things will operate. Generally not skilled in or open to negotiation. The distortion of the primary task may be seen in imposing the right agenda/stance/doctrine as determined by those with ability to impose it.

Methods for change: Focus on spiritual practice rather than content/doctrine. Educate about the norms, what they are and how to engage, while building a critical mass of parishioners who engage those practices. Encourage development of rule of life, sense of parish's position in context of broader church, world. Skill building in areas of active listening, paraphrasing, itemized response, choices for negotiation and conflict management.

**Examples of Careful Culture:** Low energy, little excitement around parish life. Sense that the place is "nice" but not really engaged in the transformative reality of the Body of Christ. Parish may seem stagnant but pleasant. Parishioners may experience sense of taking on lots of tasks or obligations but not accomplishing much. May emphasize duty over engagement. May be characterized by unrealistically idealized views of church life and underlying assumption that it's not OK to fight with (or even disagree with) those we love. May be opportunities for listening to the experiences of others but not for sharing how others affect us or how intentions may differ from actual impact. The distortion of primary task of the church may become creating a sense of comfort and belonging at the expense of spiritual, personal, and community maturity. Methods for change: Provide structured opportunity for building the capacity for Reflection. Provide opportunities for productive conflict management at lower-levels of conflict, opportunities for negotiation.

**Examples of Fear-Based Culture:** May be more likely in parishes that emphasize rules more than norms, that may emphasize "shoulds" more than they emphasize individual responsibility for spiritual life in the context of tradition and community. Underlying belief that differences will be punished. Limited structures for individual members to share their views with others or to experience positive, effective influence. Distortion of the primary task may be see in the church becoming mostly about providing structure, setting the rules, establishing consequences from outside and above, and disconnecting from a sense of personal responsibility and the demands of individual conscience. Methods for change: Collapse destructive triangles that perpetuate gossip and blame. Talk to the people responsible for whatever you're upset about. Focus on what you can do to improve the situation. Learn about the Benedictine "no grumbling" norm (discussed later on in this chapter). Become more aware of your own preferences and views. Build your competence in worship, give yourself opportunities for choice in personal participation.

One interesting aspect of this model is that the two elements, Candor and Openness, eventually merge back in on themselves and become two sides of the same coin. The highest level of communication the model describes—Collaborative— demonstrates the point at which Candor (telling the whole truth without withholding) becomes Openness.

That may seem mushy, but it's just another example of polarity. Telling "the whole truth" requires us to acknowledge we don't *possess* the whole truth and we must therefore listen openly and non-judgmentally to really understand. In this way, Collaborative communication is a polarity to be managed. True Candor requires Openness, which leads back to Candor, which demands Openness, which depends on Candor, and so on. Collaborative communication will take place as an ongoing cycle between the two poles.

It is also true that at any given point our expression of Candor might be experienced as insensitivity, aggressiveness, or steamrolling. Similarly, Openness may be experienced as passivity, indecision, and risk aversion. Each pole needs to call out the best elements of the other to be truly effective.

The model on the prior pages describes each culture resulting from the combination of higher and lower levels or Candor and Openness. In the Appendix to this book, there is some more information on the different cultures and specific suggestions for shifting your own behavior from within each of the cultural dynamics described.

## Being the community we seek

Both True Community and Collaborative Culture are most likely to grow and thrive where the members are willing to bring their real selves to the table—flawed, broken, and vulnerable; competent, brave, and compassionate—and to submit both themselves and their notions of the broader group to communal listening processes and to the sources of authority in that faith community.

In *Seeking God: The Way of St. Benedict*, Esther de Waal writes:

> The very first word of the Rule is 'listen.' From the start the disciple's goal is to hear keenly and sensitively that Word of God which is not only message but event and encounter. This is the start of a life-long process of learning, and the whole of the monastery is set out as a school of the Lord's service, a place and a structure to encourage the dialogue of master and disciple, in which the ability to listen is fundamental...

> To listen attentively to what we hear is much more than giving it passing aural attention. It means in the first instance that we have to listen whether we like it or not, whether we hear what we want to or something that is actually disagreeable or threatening. If we begin to pick and choose we are in fact turning a deaf ear to the many unexpected and perhaps unacceptable ways in which God is trying to reach us.

She goes on in a later discussion of authority to say:

> What St. Benedict expects from his abbot, as from his monks, is obedience, listening to the Word, to the Rule, to the brothers. So from the first his power is curtailed, for no dictator can emerge from a person earthed in the demands made by true obedience.

Part of our jobs as members of the church is to notice when we are listening and when we aren't. We are called to notice how the community is led, to offer support and encouragement to those charged with leadership, to be receptive, and on occasion and to name it when leaders or other members take us down a path disconnected from our primary purpose.

Does much of the energy of the parish get diverted into taking care of the most anxious members? Are we paralyzed by the idea of change?

Bob Gallagher, picking up on a phrase he got from *New York Times* columnist Nicholas Kristof, talks about "well-meaning worriers." These folks express anxiety about what *might* happen, how others *might* react, and may prevent useful change through the paralyzing effect of their concern. Even in cases where concern about reactivity is realistic, the well-meaning worriers can prevent the parish from even starting to engage the issues. To what extent do they determine, directly or indirectly, what happens and what doesn't in the parish? To what extent is each of us a well-meaning worrier?

Do we passively rely on the clergy to tell us what to do, or conversely, argue with or sabotage the clergy whenever they push our buttons? Are we instead able to appreciate and develop our healthiest inclinations, even when that causes us to confront our fears, our loneliness and our profound needs for control?

St. Benedict makes clear that once a decision has been made in accordance with the norms of the community, all should "obey cheerfully," and refrain from "murmuring in words…[or] heart." If you are anything like me, you recoil at this notion and may begin imagining all sorts of dire consequences. Indeed I have been aware of priests who, consciously or not, in both subtle and crude ways, make use of the "no grumbling" norm in Benedictine spirituality as an instrument of despotism. To do so, however, is to willfully misunderstand the nature of obedience and of truly listening and discerning in community. It is also, at least in my experience of Episcopal Church clergy, not very common.

The rector, the vestry, or other leadership groups will ultimately make a number of decisions for the community. That is their job, and to talk about the importance of listening is not to say that those decisions will or should be made "democratically." Much in the church should simply not be subject to a vote, and appropriate use of hierarchy and the resulting use of power and influence within that hierarchy is not the same as dictatorship.

Benedict understood the critical role of the leader, and he also understood the importance of the community being open to the leader, and of the leader "being earthed in the demands made by true obedience." To be effective, there must be receptivity to working together in different roles, and processes in place to allow us to listen to ourselves and one another.

For individual members of the parish, the focus is most usefully on evaluating our own participation, our own understanding of the purposes of the church, our own issues with authority figures, and developing awareness of and methods for managing our anxieties, as well as skill in interacting with others. We can learn to further the aims of the community while retaining our own sense of integrity, rather than assuming our anxieties, our needs, our preferences, should determine the outcomes for everyone else.

## Practicing community in daily life

While this chapter has focused on the special character of the church community, our lives are structured around numerous communities, formal and informal. Our workplaces, our families, our time with friends and volunteer groups, our time at church—all areas of our lives that involve joining together with others—are, for Christians, real structures of community.

Contrary to some of the messages we may hear that the best (or only) way to be a Christian in the world is to talk explicitly about Jesus or to otherwise "witness" to those around us, taking seriously Christian community requires us to accept the radical notion that in our baptism we have died with Christ and share in his resurrection, that we are members of the Body of Christ in all we do, with everyone we encounter, and that we are called to seek and serve Christ in all persons.

To the extent we have become like Christ, to the extent we have become light, salt, leaven, we will be light, salt, and leaven in the world. A key part of our job in the church is to deepen awareness of the connection between our renewal in the parish church and our apostolate in the world.

It is also part of our job to foster social connections among church members. Is coffee hour well-attended and enjoyable, with good coffee and food, and ample time to catch up with friends? Do educational events include time for connecting? Or is social activity seen as frivolous or unimportant? Are you encouraged to ignore the people you know at coffee hour and focus only on newcomers?

A healthy parish community will provide *both* opportunities to deepen and enjoy our existing relationships, and opportunities to welcome the stranger. We get off track when we forget that there is not a single answer to the "problem" of attending to our own needs and those of others. Rather we need to struggle with managing the polarities and engaging the tension among conflicting demands.

## AREAS FOR REFLECTION

- ❑ Reflect on images of the sort of church community you want to be part of. How would it look like the community you're in? How would it look different? Do you have any specific thoughts or feelings about some of the images presented in quotations in this chapter?

- ❑ Review M. Scott Peck's stages of community. Where would you put your own parish? Why? What role do you play in supporting that stage?

- ❑ Review the model describing communication and parish culture. What quadrant would you put yourself in? Where would you put your parish? Why? What communication styles do you and/or your parish employ (or not employ) that support that stage?

- ❑ Do you find yourself being a "well-meaning worrier"? Do you see that dynamic with others in the parish, or with groups you are a part of? What is the impact on community life?

- ❑ Consider your own role in the community. Is there a particular stance you take—e.g., devil's advocate, caretaker, truth-teller, strong, silent type—and if so, how does it help or hinder the development of the community you seek?

- ❑ How do you react to people you disagree with or when things don't go your way? For instance, do you think tolerance is an important virtue but become dismissive and angry with people in your church who have different political beliefs from you? If the church chooses to do something you don't like, do you refuse to participate? Gather evidence in the parking lot that others share your views?

- ❑ Notice responsibilities or duties you take on that you find burdensome or that cause you resentment. Is there a change you could make that would allow you to share the responsibility or to see the responsibility differently? What would be the consequences of letting it go entirely?

❑ Are there duties you've accepted that you don't follow through on or perform adequately? Are others "chasing" you to get things done? What are the consequences for you and for the community?

❑ What is your own relationship to authority? What are the forms of authority you value the most? The least? How does this play out in your life?

## Ways to Experiment with Participation in Community

- ❑ Pay attention to the experience of visitors to your church. What do you notice? What is your own experience of social time at church? If you typically don't speak to visitors, consider deciding to have a brief conversation with one person you don't know. If you normally devote a great deal of energy to newcomers, consider arranging to step back one Sunday and spend time with your friends.

- ❑ Adopt a "no grumbling" or "no whining" stance as a form of spiritual discipline. Commit to this stance for a month and spend some time each week reflecting on how that feels, whether you're able to do it, what it's like if you are able to and what it's like if you aren't able to. Do you sense any difference between accommodation and acceptance?

- ❑ Try a new behavior in a group you participate in. For instance, if you often play devil's advocate, try consciously relinquishing that role. Generate curiosity about what options might be available to you if you change your habitual behavior. Reflect on how that felt, what worked well, what didn't. What might you try in the future?

- ❑ Experiment with letting your yes be yes and your no be no. Think carefully before agreeing to do something or refusing to do something and then respond honestly and unequivocally. How would your experience be different if you were fully committed to things you agree to do, or if you stopped taking on duties you don't want?

- ❑ Experiment with renegotiating commitments. You may have agreed to something and others now depend on you. You find you can't or don't want to do what you have agreed to do. See if you can openly enter into a discussion about your dilemma, without assuming the outcome. Assume you may end up continuing with the commitment, doing it in some revised manner, agreeing to do something in its place, or be relieved of the responsibility.

COMMUNITY LIFE ASSESSMENT

## Images of the Community

**1. The community I seek** is one in which people are free to be themselves; to speak and listen fully and authentically. In which differences are accepted (we can fight with those we love). In which we can make decisions and solve the problems we face.

| I don't want church to be that way | | | | It is what I seek; and more |
|---|---|---|---|---|
| 1 | 2 | 3 | 4 | 5 |

## 2. Connection with people

| I don't know anyone well | | | | I know a number of people and have a few friends in the parish |
|---|---|---|---|---|
| 1 | 2 | 3 | 4 | 5 |

## 3. Participation in parish social life

| Not at all | | | | I participate regularly and frequently |
|---|---|---|---|---|
| 1 | 2 | 3 | 4 | 5 |

**4. Listening in community** requires listening to one another "whether we like it or not, whether we hear what we want to or something that is actually disagreeable or threatening." (From *Seeking God: The Way of St. Benedict,* by Esther DeWaal)

| I don't want church to be that way | | | | It is what I seek; and more |
|---|---|---|---|---|
| 1 | 2 | 3 | 4 | 5 |

**5.** Once a **decision** has been made in accordance with the norms of the community, I work at being supportive. "All should obey cheerfully and...refrain from "murmuring in words...[or] heart." (From *The Rule of St. Benedict.*)

| I don't want church to be that way | | | | It is what I seek; and more |
|---|---|---|---|---|
| 1 | 2 | 3 | 4 | 5 |

**Assess your own participation in the parish community**

**6. I frequently find myself** agreeing with others at church, or simply remaining silent, because I don't want to cause conflict.

| This is very true for me. | | | | This is not true—I may generate conflict for its own sake. |
|---|---|---|---|---|
| 1 | 2 | 3 | 4 | 5 |

## 7. On speaking fully and authentically.

| I avoid saying what I think if I believe others will be upset | | I carefully consider my words and their impact on people, but generally share feelings and opinions I think are important | | I say what I want, when and how I want to say it, with little prior consideration of how others will feel. |
|---|---|---|---|---|
| 1 | 2 | 3 | 4 | 5 |

## 8. How I manage commitments I make in the parish. (Circle the pattern that comes closest)

| I often take on duties I don't want and then fail to complete them | I take things on I don't want and complete them. | If I take too much on I am good at renegotiating commitments in a timely manner | I am pretty good at only agreeing to what I'm able and willing to do. | I am pretty good at knowing what I'm able and willing to do. I'm willing on occasion to stretch beyond that for the community. |
|---|---|---|---|---|

*One's first duty is adoration, and one's second duty is awe and only one's third duty is service. And that for those three things and nothing else, addressed to God and no one else, you and I and countless human creatures evolved...We observe then that two of the three things for which our souls were made are matters of attitude, or relation: adoration and awe. Unless these two are right, the last of the triad, service, won't be right.*

**Evelyn Underhill, *Concerning the Inner Life***

*All around us, to right and left, in front and behind, above and below, we have only to go a little beyond the frontier of sensible appearances in order to see the divine welling up and showing through. But it is not only close to us, in front of us, that the divine presence has revealed itself. It has sprung up universally, and we find ourselves so surrounded and transfixed by it, that there is no room left to fall down and adore it, even within ourselves.*

*By means of all created things, without exception, the divine assails us, penetrates us and moulds us. We imagined it as distant and inaccessible, whereas in fact we live steeped in its burning layers. In eo vivimus. As Jacob said, awakening from his dream, the world, this palpable world, which we were wont to treat with the boredom and disrespect with which we habitually regard places with no sacred association for us, is in truth a holy place, and we did not know it.*

**Pierre Teilhard de Chardin**

# Six

# Service

Here is my sad confession: when talk of Christian service comes up, I often feel guilty and irritated. Guilty because I'm not doing enough, sacrificing the way I should, suffering as much as I could. Irritated because it seems so easy to exhort people to do *more*, and because such exhortations embody for me much of the worst sort of self-righteous religiosity. Which then makes me feel guilty again because I'm clearly just too lazy, not to mention insincere in my faith, to do the right thing and instead expend my energy on negative thoughts.

In many ways, these reactions are little more than my own sort of circular agitation, focused on what isn't working rather than on what is. If I take the time to pay attention instead of judging, all around me I see the myriad ways we serve. I can then come back to my understanding that for most Christians our primary service is found in the activities of daily life.

We serve others in our families, with our friends, at work, in the places we volunteer, in our participation in civic life, and sometimes even in our churches. Most of us won't quit our jobs and head off to work in the slums of Calcutta, or even minister in the streets with the homeless of our own cities. But all of us have real opportunities every day to see Christ in our neighbors and to reflect the light of Christ in our routine interactions and decisions.

Our judgments about what service should be, our commitment to grand gestures, can inspire us to do important things. But often, they get in the way of figuring out or even noticing what we are called to do in our lives, every day, as they actually are. Those judgments distract our attention from what we are already doing and prevent our being able to listen with an open heart to our longings for integrity and wholeness in Christ.

For each of us to take seriously the stuff of our daily lives would have significant impact in the world. But it is also scary precisely because it is realistic and attainable, and because it also requires being buried with Christ each and every day, often without any obvious reminder that we also share in His resurrection. I know that both death and resurrection are with us always, but death can be much easier to recognize and to run from.

In considering service, the first place to start is with the rest of this book. The right relationship with God is interwoven with the right relationship with others. That means that we really do need to pay attention to our own renewal, our opportunities for worship and connection with God and the people we care about. These things aren't luxuries or afterthoughts and making them a priority will have significant positive consequences for the ways we live as Christians, and therefore the ways we serve God and his creation.

It's also helpful to spend more time focused on the power and influence we currently wield. Instead of bemoaning the state of the world, or even of the city, we would do better to recognize those areas in our own lives where we can realistically make changes, or influence others to make changes.

We also need to think about the wider world, but it doesn't do anyone any good to dismiss the smaller problems in front of us in deference to the enormity of the world's suffering.

## Work life

We may sometimes get the impression that the only "Christian" work is in the church itself or related to direct service to the poor. In fact, though, Christian work is that work done faithfully and conscientiously by Christians. I am not saying that good intentions conquer inherent evil—a slumlord refusing heat to his tenants in winter while praying that God will one day give them better housing does not represent "work done faithfully and conscientiously," although it may be faithful to the goals of the average slumlord.

It's tricky. There are, after all, some folks who would say that oil companies are inherently evil—and that, by extension, the people employed by them are doing evil work—but most of them still drive cars or take airplanes or buses, which I think weakens the argument a bit. If oil is necessary, or at least useful, then oil companies are, too, and the people who work for them are providing a service.

If you accept that premise, then it becomes possible to consider a whole host of more interesting questions. What are the obligations of an oil company to the environment? To the local and international economy? To its employees? To future generations? To its shareholders (who, of course, may well be decent Christians who rely on oil-company dividends to feed their families and make charitable contributions)?

This last example became a significant problem after BP Oil's rig explosion and consequent disastrous spill in the Gulf of Mexico in 2010. Amid demands that BP suspend its dividend and redirect that money to clean up of the spill, came counter-demands that the government protect pension funds and individual investors heavily reliant on exactly those dividends.

And of course, no company acts on its own. While corporations are legally "persons," they don't actually exist apart from the people who run them. *All* corporate actions are undertaken by the entity's employees, officers, directors or agents. If those individuals recognize their own accountability for corporate actions, then it becomes much more likely that individual conscience and the proper use of individual power and influence will find greater sway.

Rhetoric about "evil, nameless corporations" has the unfortunate consequence of both permitting corporate employees to dismiss this ranting as unfair and ill-informed, and allowing distancing from the real-world consequences of corporate decision-making.

### It's not about explicit religiosity

Wherever we work, we have opportunities to decide how we will treat our customers, our co-workers, the people we supervise. We have choices to make about compensation, about policies and procedures, about our corporate ethics. For religious people, our faith should inform those decisions and guide us in building a work environment that has integrity. This is not about telling everybody we work with they need to accept Jesus Christ as their personal savior. It is about baptized persons taking seriously the services we provide, the different stakeholders we are accountable to, and being willing to deal head-on with those places where we can do better.

Many years ago I was hired to help with the turnaround of a brokerage firm that had been founded on the basis of shared faith. Most of the brokers, and all of the home office employees, were evangelical Christians. The company was run with a widespread assumption that actual supervision of the brokers wasn't really necessary, specifically because of the religious commonality.

When I came on board, the firm was fighting crippling lawsuits resulting from some rogue brokers who had sold fraudulent investments without the consent or knowledge of the company. Even though the firm did not know about or approve of these investments, the law tended to favor the investors by saying that the firm was liable for the conduct of its agents if it knew *or should have known* what they were doing.

Our lawyers encouraged us to defend ourselves and to vigorously deny all responsibility, while emphasizing the bad decisions made by the investors themselves. In some ways, we had no choice because the losses involved were far bigger than the firm's assets. To admit liability could have immediately bankrupted the firm.

Yet the president of the company, who was also an evangelical Christian, struggled with the fact that he believed the clients had been harmed and that the firm's prior *laissez-faire* attitude toward its very religious brokers had probably contributed to the problem. Eventually, he decided to approach the plaintiffs directly and talk about what had happened. He explained our role, what we knew, what we didn't know, what we could have done better. He also explained that the firm had limited assets and that losing these lawsuits would put the company out of business and generate little or nothing for the plaintiffs.

He also made it clear that he thought the investors had been wronged and that our company had in some way made that possible. He had to word this carefully because our insurance carrier was extremely reluctant to admit any wrongdoing. He offered to work with the plaintiffs to try to recover money from the brokers and the companies that had issued the bad investments and suggested that the firm could reallocate some legal fees to this effort rather than to defending itself.

From a business standpoint, the approach "worked" in that the investors stopped fighting with us. It could just as easily have backfired because we took a significant risk in acknowledging the company's role—albeit one of omission—in the problem. What it did ensure was that the people working for the company felt they were doing something worthwhile that didn't require them to compromise their basic beliefs.

Interestingly, the other significant thing the president did was to stop having company meetings and policies focused on explicitly Christian values and statements. Instead, he focused the company on competent and professional provision of financial services. He implemented new standards of conduct, required additional training, and insisted that all brokers submit to rigorous oversight, no matter what church they attended or how many Bible quotes they included in their client meetings.

By working to ensure that the company offered investment products and advice in an appropriate and professional way—rather than in a "Christian" way—he did far more to ensure that the company actually operated in a manner consistent with its religious ideals.

## Civic life

Most of us won't run for office or create a grass-roots community change effort, but we can stay informed about the current issues and we can make sure we vote, talk to others, give money where that makes sense, serve on juries, and pay our taxes.

Even these basic ways of participating in civic life can seem too much at times. That's where it's important to accept responsibility for creating some form of discipline around what we consider the minimal requirements.

The county I live in recently switched to all mail-in ballots. While I understood the need to cut costs and that eliminating polling places may make it easier for a wider group of people to participate, I found the change a little sad. What I eventually realized, though, was that the change could foster a deeper degree of involvement, which I had not expected.

A friend told me that when she first looked at the ballot, she knew almost none of the names of people running for mayor, county council, or school board, and she had no clue about any of the propositions on the ballot. She felt tired and wanted to just let the due date pass without mailing in the ballot, but her sense of civic duty kicked in and she decided to spend half an hour figuring it out.

She got on-line, looked up the candidate statements, read some endorsements, and reviewed the voter's guide. In the end, she thought she had a pretty good sense of how she should vote. She also realized that had she simply gone to the polls, she would have checked off a couple of the ballot items and then ignored the rest, simply because she didn't know enough.

While this seems like a small thing, my friend believes that a minimal involvement in civic life is required of her as a Christian and as a citizen. That belief, coupled with a willingness to confront her own inconsistencies, helped her create greater integrity in this area of her life.

Similarly, when I was called for jury duty recently, I realized it was going to be inconvenient for me both professionally and personally. But that was it: inconvenient, not fatal. My company had experienced some success in getting people excused and I got a little pressure to try that from my boss. My response was to say that I thought it was an important responsibility and that I valued the fact that the company supported its employees' efforts to serve. That was enough. Nobody bugged me about it further and several people pitched in to make sure my job was covered. I was out for a week, which required sacrifices from a few people, but it was also for me an important thing to do as a member of this community.

### Family and friends

Our relationships with family and friends provide a unique opportunity to be fully who we are now, to appreciate the intimacy we share with those we are closest to, and to create a space to enter into what we are becoming. Our service to family and friends is a key part of Christian identity.

Most of us have a natural inclination to devote energy and time to our families. We are also formed by our families in a profound way, and the power of those relationships can be a path toward transforming our daily lives into something that truly reflects the Kingdom of God. Caring for a sick parent, child, spouse, or friend; bringing over food after the birth of a child or the death of a spouse;

In a similar way, our friends know us and love us but they don't usually carry the same baggage that we have with our families (something perhaps aided by the fact that they don't usually have to go home with us). The tolerance we feel for a friend's idiosyncrasies; the opportunities for forgiveness and acceptance that present themselves all too frequently; time spent sharing common passions and deepening our capacities for pursuing what we love; opportunities to care for the sick; the chance to be told honestly and lovingly that we've screwed up, or to accept that we are genuinely loved—these are the place where we grow up in Christ.

In my own family, I have learned that I am not a naturally fabulous mother, either in terms of being a lot of fun or of being devoted and selfless. I love and like my son, but I don't much like video games or sports or noise. I am also more self-centered and more jealously protective of my free time than is seemly for a modern parent. Finally, I am also an unusually skilled justifier of *what I want*.

As I have been willing to more honestly examine the implications of being a Christian and a parent, I have also had to confront the selfishness that has been present in my relationship with my son. I am not perfect by any stretch, but I have taken concrete steps to engage my son in ways that are not about my preferences but are about modeling for him what I value and what I believe to be right. They are also about a willingness to accept my son for who he is and to embrace the stuff he cares about (at least a little) because it really isn't all about me, much as I often wish it were.

Others are able to find in family life a natural extension of the familial images present in the church. The family becomes the primary place they experience the love of God and the sense that they have been endowed with a special creative capacity, fluidly nurturing and easily reflecting the kingdom of heaven in the microcosm of family life.

## Some interesting stuff with non-religious friends

Outside of Seattle, almost all my friends are Episcopalians who are serious about their spiritual life. With my Seattle friends, I am frequently the only one in the group who is religious. Most members of my immediate family are not active in the church.

Contrary to what we might be taught, this difference is seldom an opportunity for explicit evangelization, nor is it an indication that anything is inherently lacking in the relationship. It is, though, often an opportunity for genuine service in some specific ways.

Non-religious people often struggle with a forum for discussing their spiritual doubts and fears. They have a spiritual life but they are not part of a spiritual community or tradition and so they may have to work harder to discern the questions that are a natural backdrop to religious life.

By taking spiritual questions seriously, and sometimes by providing information about the language I use, the practices followed by my community, and the perspectives we share, I am occasionally able to provide valuable structure to the other person's journey. I don't tell them what to do or what to believe, but I do provide information about spiritual traditions.

In many cases this provides non-religious people additional choices and also may offer an opportunity to see the church as something other than merely oppressive or judgmental or irrelevant. Most important, it encourages people who are in a different place to take their own spiritual lives seriously and to recognize that they're not really alone.

## Death and secular life

This may be particularly applicable when looking at how modern society deals with death. Lauren Winner, in her lovely book *Mud House Sabbath: An Invitation to a Life of Spiritual Discipline*, describes Jewish traditions around death and mourning. She explains the way they are connected to the rhythms of life, how specific time periods are marked and acknowledged, and how the rituals correspond with the varying levels of incapacity we feel depending on where we are in the grieving process.

Initially, we're a mess. After a week, we need to start doing some things while acknowledging the loss we've experienced. After a year, life is more normal, but we don't forget. On some level, mourning continues for the rest of our lives but we also take specific steps to carry out our obligations and not lose our own capacity for life in the depths of grief.

I shared this section of the book with my non-religious friend, David, who had experienced his friend Tyler's traumatic death a year earlier. David was struck by how much the book spoke to his own needs and how helpful it might be to have some concrete rituals and expectations around how to mourn.

There had been several memorial-service-type events after Tyler's death, but the overall purpose seemed unclear. They were almost entirely unstructured, almost exclusively party-oriented, and the timing was unusual: as soon as one event was over, the next would be planned. The last of these took place about six months after Tyler's death, with the promise that there would be another on the anniversary. While my view may not jibe with those closest to Tyler, for me the impact was to delay the inevitable process of dealing with the terrible reality of life without Tyler. Who am I and what is my life like without this person?

David's uncle, Eric, died unexpectedly shortly after our conversation about *Mudhouse Sabbath*. This was a significant personal loss for David and, because of the circumstances, he was forced to remain highly task-oriented, making arrangements for other family members and attending to his uncle's property. He went through periods of intense grief, but also remained highly focused on doing what he had to do.

Other family members, who come from a religious tradition but recognized that Eric was not practicing, arranged a mostly non-religious memorial service about two weeks later. It included reminiscence, music, poetry, a sense of Eric's values and purpose, and an acknowledgement that everyone present was grieving and that they would also be returning to their own lives in the wake of this loss.

David commented after the service that he felt like someone had taken a heavy boot off his chest. He felt sad but he also felt relieved and as if he had reached a new stage in his own mourning.

There were certainly a number of important differences between Tyler and Eric, the manner of their deaths, and among the cultural norms and range of acceptable behaviors for the people most intimately involved. Nonetheless, it also seemed that engaging life in a structured way while finding rituals for both mourning and marking the end of deepest mourning, provided significant value. These structures and rituals come out of a religious approach to life, even when their content is not explicitly religious. Sharing them generously can be a valuable form of service.

### The meaning of friendship

The prior paragraphs contain a lot of spiritual language in reference to friendship and I do not want to inadvertently imply that friendship is primarily a dry religious duty, a stealthy technique for bringing others to Christ, or somehow important only when addressing a specifically spiritual concern. A quote from C.S. Lewis gets at the issue for me: "Friendship is unnecessary, like philosophy, like art... It has no survival value; rather it is one of those things that give value to survival."

Friendship is so central, so much a part of how my life is constructed, that it is difficult to tease out how it reflects service separate from how it reflects plain old living. Joy, pain, anger, ennui, working hard, relaxing—each of these is less sustainable or less bearable when experienced without friends.

The ornithologist, Edward W. Howe, said, "When a friend is in trouble, don't annoy him by asking if there is anything you can do. Think up something appropriate and do it."

## QUESTIONS FOR REFLECTION

❑ Where is it that you find yourself making a contribution to the welfare of humanity? Where are you aware of being an instrument of God's love? [9]

  - In my family
  - With friends
  - In the work I do
  - In my relationship with co-workers
  - In volunteer work I do
  - In working with a civic group or community organization
  - Other?

❑ How has being part of the church helped or hindered this?

❑ Are there areas of your life that seem particularly congruent or incongruent with your faith? How is that expressed? Some areas to think about are your work life, relationships with friends and family, use of money, use of time, role of sex, and attitude toward the secular world.

---

[9] Question from The Renewal—Apostolate Cycle, *Fill All Things: The Dynamics of Spirituality in the Parish Church,* © 2008, Robert A. Gallagher, Ascension Press

*Personal petition is the heart of prayer just as corporate adoration is its peak. It is unfortunate that Protestantism tends so to stress the value of petition—"sincere prayer from the heart"—that it obscures its ultimate consummation in the corporate worship of the Church. It is just as regrettable that a certain type of Catholicism so emphasizes the Office and the Eucharist that it overlooks a personal religion which alone guarantees adequate participation in them. All of which argument and schism is done away once we recognize the place of each in the patterned process of the rule of the Church. For the "heart" of private prayer I mean, in this instance, the source of personal love which flows throughout the Mystical Body.*

**Martin Thornton, *Christian Proficiency***

# Seven

# The Process of Spiritual Growth

This is the end of the book.[10]  In the preceding chapters, I have tried to make concrete and useful some of the spiritual practices that have sustained the Christian tradition.  Here is where I try to integrate the whole shebang and help you create a Rule of Life.

As mentioned in the introduction, in writing this book (and Bob Gallagher's companion book) we wanted to avoid the Bunch O' Cool Practices approach to spiritual life and make sure that we were offering a *system*.  A system both grounded in Christian tradition and reflecting the realities of modern life.

The map that appears at the beginning of the book, as well as the specific practices described throughout the book, are the disciplines developed by the Church.  They represent a relatively broad view of Christian tradition as particularly expressed in the Anglican Church.

A Rule of Life is the means by which individual Christians establish an intentional pattern of spiritual discipline.  It will broadly contain the elements of Weekly Practice, Daily Practice, Reflectiveness, Community Participation, and Service, but will also be tailored to your individual circumstances.

The idea is that a Rule of Life will be robust enough to sustain your spiritual life over time, but flexible enough to be reflected on, revised, and deepened.  You should feel some stretch, but not excessive burden.  You should be able to follow the Rule in the ordinary circumstances of your life.

We have included a numbers of assessments and worksheets for you to use in developing your own Rule of Life.  It might be helpful to start with the overall assessment of spiritual practice

---

[10] Are you still here or have you disappeared in a poof of spiritual enlightenment?  Joke, joke!

found at the beginning of the book. Did one of the practices assessed strike you as less well-developed than the others? If so, which one? An initial form of Rule might focus on developing those practices that seem less established.

There are also several more detailed worksheets. They are similar but each has a different emphasis—try them and see what emerges.

The important thing is to develop something you actually implement. Try it and see what happens. Does some element of your new Rule need to be adjusted? Does it seem that you've taken on too much? Too little?

Pay attention to your reaction and to what you're actually doing. The parts that are easier for you will naturally form the core of your Rule. You can them experiment with different forms of the other elements to find something that works for you as an integrated system.

In developing your own spiritual discipline you might draw on some of the assumptions offered early in the book:

1. We all have a spiritual life.
2. It is a significant act of spiritual growth when we accept responsibility for our spiritual life.
3. A healthy spiritual life assumes engagement, rather than escape; an interest in the life of the world instead of spiritual sentimentality or being caught up in illusions.
4. We are seeking a spiritual practice with roots in ancient ways and useful in modern life.
5. We need a spirituality that is both solid and resilient.
6. Our spiritual life serves us best when we understand that it is to evolve over time. What serves us when we are 11 differs from when we are 18 and still again from when we are 35 or 60. A fruitful evolution arises out of forms of spiritual life that are complex, rich, and paradoxical. They continue to grow as we increase our self-awareness, insight, and in response to changing circumstances.
7. It requires efficiency if it is to serve modern daily life.

8. It requires attention and time if it is to serve modern daily life.
9. Our spiritual life and discipline is to be based on an integrated system, a pattern, rather than series of random practices. We are to live our spiritual life by Rule, not rules.
10. It is possible for the average church member to become competent and proficient in spiritual practices.
11. We must decide to base our spiritual life on persistence, courage, and competence, rather than on feelings— whether we feel like praying or not. A useful and faithful spiritual life requires critical reasoning and intelligences. We need to intentionally turn away from spiritual fads and fast food.
12. The parish church's primary task is the spiritual formation of its people.

## Rule of Life Worksheet

# The Renewal—Apostolate Cycle

The Renewal - Apostolate Cycle is a way of describing a central dynamic of Christian life. The Cycle focuses our attention on the Christian's movement between being renewed in baptismal identity and purpose and living as instruments of God's love and grace in daily life. The Cycle is interested in both the individual's movement and in the ways in which the parish church supports and facilitates that movement. This is the primary task of any parish church.

**RENEWAL**

Renewal in baptismal identity and purpose in worship, study, the parish's social life, and being equipped for Christian action

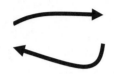

**APOSTOLATE**

Participation in the work of Christ in service, evangelization and stewardship
In areas of:
  Workplace, Civic Life,
  Family & Friends,
  Church

**A Cycle**

The cycle is between a conscious and intentional attention to God, prayer life, our relationships, Christian formation **and** a subconscious reliance upon God as members of the Body of Christ, in the workplace, family, friendship, civic life and congregational life.

**In that Cycle:**

| We need: | Which is helped by: | Which the parish helps by: |
| --- | --- | --- |
| To accept our dependence on God | Openness to spiritual guidance | An emphasis in its life on worship; nothing comes before the Eucharist and Daily Office. Also, more attention to formation and spiritual growth than other programs or ministries. |
| To accept responsibility for ordering our spiritual life | Establishing a rule of life | Offering programs and guidance in creating, experimenting with, and revising a spiritual discipline. |
| To accept our interdependence with others in the Church | Life in Christian community, a parish church | Being a healthy and faithful parish church and by helping people relate to the parish community in ways appropriate to their personality and the parish's capacities. Having opportunities for social life and the development of friendships. |

From *Fill All Things: The Spiritual Dynamics of the Parish Church,* © Robert A Gallagher, 2008

**Reflection**
Make notes for yourself.

1. How are you renewed in your baptismal identity and purpose?

2. How do you renew yourself emotionally and physically?

3. How do you get in the way of your own renewal?

- baptismal renewal

- emotional/physical renewal

4. How do you live your apostolate in an active way? (note specific patterns of behavior, commitments, etc.). There is no assumption her that you should have a response for each area. You may be more focused on a way of being present in all of life or you may have a more intense calling in one area rather than another

- family

- with friends

- workplace

- civic life

- church

## Change & Experimentation

1. What do you want to experiment with to improve your own Renewal-Apostolate Cycle?

2. Note anything specific you want to experiment with related to receiving spiritual guidance

3. Note anything you want to experiment with in relationship to your participation in the Eucharistic community (the parish).

4. Note anything you want to experiment with in a rule of prayer (Mass – Office – Personal Devotions)

Copyright Robert A. Gallagher 2005, 2006

## Worksheet: Balancing Life by the Rule

Based on Debra Farrington's "Balancing Life by the Rule in Spirituality & Health 2001

**1. Make a list of all the things you do that nurture your spirit.**

## 2. Relate your list from item 1 to the eight categories listed in the second column. Circle the one that applies.

| Things that nurture your spirit | Use this column in step #2 | |
|---|---|---|
| | - Seeking God<br>- Work<br>- Study<br>- Spiritual community | - Worship<br>- Care of your body<br>- Reaching out<br>- Hospitality |
| | - Seeking God<br>- Work<br>- Study<br>- Spiritual community | - Worship<br>- Care of your body<br>- Reaching out<br>- Hospitality |
| | - Seeking God<br>- Work<br>- Study<br>- Spiritual community | - Worship<br>- Care of your body<br>- Reaching out<br>- Hospitality |
| | - Seeking God<br>- Work<br>- Study<br>- Spiritual community | - Worship<br>- Care of your body<br>- Reaching out<br>- Hospitality |
| | - Seeking God<br>- Work<br>- Study<br>- Spiritual community | - Worship<br>- Care of your body<br>- Reaching out<br>- Hospitality |
| | - Seeking God<br>- Work<br>- Study<br>- Spiritual community | - Worship<br>- Care of your body<br>- Reaching out<br>- Hospitality |
| | - Seeking God<br>- Work<br>- Study<br>- Spiritual community | - Worship<br>- Care of your body<br>- Reaching out<br>- Hospitality |
| | - Seeking God<br>- Work | - Worship<br>- Care of your body |

112

| | | |
|---|---|---|
| | ▪ Study<br>▪ Spiritual community | ▪ Reaching out<br>▪ Hospitality |
| | ▪ Seeking God<br>▪ Work<br>▪ Study<br>▪ Spiritual community | ▪ Worship<br>▪ Care of your body<br>▪ Reaching out<br>▪ Hospitality |
| | ▪ Seeking God<br>▪ Work<br>▪ Study<br>▪ Spiritual community | ▪ Worship<br>▪ Care of your body<br>▪ Reaching out<br>▪ Hospitality |
| | ▪ Seeking God<br>▪ Work<br>▪ Study<br>▪ Spiritual community | ▪ Worship<br>▪ Care of your body<br>▪ Reaching out<br>▪ Hospitality |
| | ▪ Seeking God<br>▪ Work<br>▪ Study<br>▪ Spiritual community | ▪ Worship<br>▪ Care of your body<br>▪ Reaching out<br>▪ Hospitality |

**3. Reflect on the work you've done. Are some of the eight areas blank? Is that because you don't think of them as part of your spiritual life?**

**4. Develop a practice of on occasion intentionally offering these activities to God.** The primary way is to offer it silently when the gifts are presented at the altar during the Eucharist. You might also develop it as a form of recollection during the day. Don't try to do it all the time – it's not possible or desirable. Allow the times you do make the offering to shape your heart and mind so a subconscious offering of your life is part of how you live.

## Creating Your Spiritual Discipline Worksheet
## Current Practices

The Anglican tradition assumes that adults are responsible for their own spiritual life; for shaping their own rule of life. This is grounded in the state of being that exists by having been baptized into the Body of Christ. We develop our rule by accepting responsibility and drawing on the resources and tradition of the wider church. So, we take into account the church's threefold rule of prayer and ways in which we may best receive spiritual guidance.

You are invited to make use of these two worksheets in reflecting on your spiritual discipline. This first worksheet is about the ways in which you currently are renewed.

|  | Current Practices |
|---|---|
| How I am renewed emotionally and physically. |  |
| Participation in the Holy Eucharist |  |
| Participation in the Daily Prayers of the Church |  |
| Ways of being reflective |  |

| | |
|---|---|
| Participation in the Community | |
| Being equipped for Christian action. | |
| Study of Scripture, theology, etc. | |
| Other | |

---

## Creating Your Spiritual Discipline Worksheet
## Practices to Explore & Try Out

This second worksheet is to help you in identifying revisions to your practice; ways in which you may want to experiment. Make notes in each area. If possible share what you are thinking with your spiritual director or others whose counsel you value.

|  | Things to Explore or Try |
| --- | --- |
| How I am renewed emotionally and physically. |  |
| Participation in the Holy Eucharist |  |
| Participation in the Daily Prayers of the Church |  |
| Ways of being reflective |  |
| Participation in the Community |  |
| Being equipped for Christian action. |  |

| | |
|---|---|
| Study of Scripture, theology, etc. | |
| Other | |

## Establishing a Rule of Life
## Christian Life Model

A rule of life is the means by which an individual Christian establishes an intentional pattern of Christian discipline which can over time, be reflected upon, revised, and deepened. Your rule is an expression of the faith and practice of the whole church in your own life; a discipline freely taken on to give order, support, and direction to your life. It is a means of rooting your life in Christ.

As each of us is unique, so each rule will have a somewhat different shape. However, every rule needs to have as its base and starting point the Anglican tradition's threefold rule of prayer (Holy Eucharist, Daily Office, and Personal Devotions) and expression of the Christian life in worship, doctrine and action. This helps us to give ourselves to an integrated pattern of life that is grounded in the larger Christian experience, rather than to make up our own list of "rules" to follow.

You might use the worksheet once to note what you already are doing, then a second time to note what you would like to try doing now. Be specific and realistic. Rules change with time and circumstance.

A. WORSHIP: *Continue ...in the breaking of the bread and the prayers.*

1. Holy Eucharist – Participation on all Sundays and Major Holy Days

2. Daily Office - which Office? When? How? With whom?

3. Personal Devotions – Intercession and/or recollection and/or meditation and/or...

4.   Spiritual Reading

5.   Other

**B. DOCTRINE:**   *Continue in the apostle's teaching and fellowship*
Connecting yourself with what has authority in the Christian
Life. Increasing your ability to relate those sources of authority to
your decision-making; understanding how to use Scripture –
Tradition – Reason as you reflect on your life and as a backdrop
in discernment and decision making.

1.   Scripture—*lectio divina* and/or study. Consider relating
     this to use of the Daily Office

2.   Christian doctrine, church history, ethics

3.   Other

**C. ACTION:**   *To represent Christ and his church; to bear witness to him
wherever they may be*
Describe your responsibilities and opportunities for service,
evangelization and stewardship in the various areas of your life.

1.   Family

2.   Friends

3.   Work

4.   Community – Neighborhood – as a citizen

5.   Church

6.   Self

## The Christian Life Model

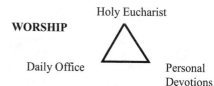

WORSHIP — Holy Eucharist — Daily Office — Personal Devotions

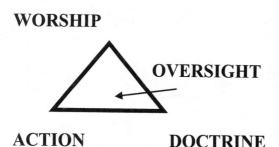

WORSHIP — OVERSIGHT — ACTION — DOCTRINE

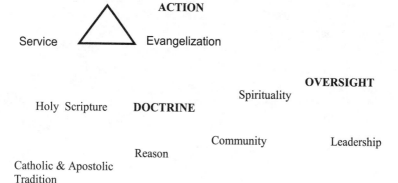

ACTION — Stewardship — Service — Evangelization

DOCTRINE — Holy Scripture — Reason — Catholic & Apostolic Tradition

OVERSIGHT — Spirituality — Community — Leadership

Copyright Robert A. Gallagher 1984, 2006

120

# Appendix

## Additional Information on Communication Model

This communication model (see the chapter on Community) describes an interplay between Candor and Openness. Different combinations of lower and higher Candor and Openness result in different cultural dynamics.

In the parish church, this can be seen as a distortion of the church's primary task, with certain predictable dynamics. I have described below some additional detail about the distortions and specific practices or methods that the individual can employ to shift their own communication style.

Note that distortions of primary task may represent perfectly acceptable behaviors in isolation, but they become a distortion when the church comes to believe that these values are primary, and that they represent the core purpose of the parish. This happens more easily when parish leaders and lay people don't openly discuss what the primary task should be and how the parish does or doesn't live into that mission.

A key assumption of this book is that the primary task of the parish church is the spiritual formation of its members.

### Fear-Based Culture: *Low Candor coupled with Low Openness*

**Distortion of Primary Task:** Provide structure, set the rules, establish consequences from outside and above.

### *Possible Methods for Change*

Collapse destructive triangles that perpetuate gossip and blame. Talk to the people responsible for whatever you're upset about. Focus on what you can do to improve the situation. Learn about the Benedictine "no grumbling" norm (discussed later on in this chapter). Become more aware of your own preferences and views.

Build your competence in worship, give yourself opportunities for choice in personal participation.

**Careful Culture: *Low Candor* with *Higher Openness***

**Distortion of Primary Task:** Create sense of comfort and belonging at expense of other values.


### *Possible Methods for Change*

Develop more capacity for Reflection in community (e.g., participate in silent retreats at the parish, journaling, affinity-group opportunities, such as women's/men's spirituality) where you can draw a clear connection between experience and impact. Also engage more self-focused activities such as therapy or spiritual direction. Notice what you think or feel that you're not saying. Pay attention to underlying assumptions or beliefs that keep you from sharing your thoughts and feelings, such as, "I'll hurt her feelings," "It's not important," "I'm probably the only one who thinks this."

Build a capacity in yourself for recognizing when and why you choose to be silent and notice that as a process that will shift as you make different decisions, rather than some unchangeable force of the universe.

When you're more comfortable with your internal process, offer more self-disclosure as it seems safe and reasonable to do so. Ask for feedback about how your behavior affects others. If you think someone's feelings are hurt or if you think you might have been too aggressive, check it out with the other person. If your impact didn't match your intention, ask what you might have done differently.

Bob Gallagher, picking up on a term he got from *New York Times* columnist Nicholas Kristof, talks about "well-meaning worriers." These folks express anxiety about what *might* happen, how others *might* react, and may prevent useful change through the paralyzing effect of what may be misplaced concern. Or, even in cases where concern about reactivity is realistic, the well-meaning worriers can prevent the parish from even *starting* to engage the issues. Careful Cultures likely have a noticeable number of well-meaning worriers.

**Aggressive Culture:** *Higher Candor with Low Openness*

**Distortion of Primary Task:** Imposing the "right" agenda/stance/doctrine as determined by those who have the most power and influence.

## *Possible Methods for Change*

Focus on spiritual practice rather than emphasizing content/doctrine or perpetuating the fight. Say Compline together after a contentious meeting rather than offer individual, off-the-cuff intercessions for "tolerance" or "recognition that God is leading us down Path Y." Learn about the patterns of spiritual practice, what they are and how to engage them, while building your own competency.

Develop a rule of life and a deeper sense of your own place in the parish, the broader church, and the world. Learn about active listening and other elements of openness and find ways to practice openness—curiosity and suspension of judgment while you try to truly understand the other person. Consider a more complete response to ideas you don't like. Rather than disagree, try to identify what you like about an idea, what concerns you, and what you might want to see, such as by identifying what you like, what concerns you, and what you wish for (likes/concerns/wishes).

**Competitive Culture:** *Higher Candor with Higher Openness*

**Distortion of Primary Task:** Determining "the truth."

## *Possible Methods for Change*

Focus on spiritual practice, with an emphasis on corporate worship. Emphasize spiritual formation, skill building, explore Benedictine practices around obedience and listening. Evaluate your own skills in these areas. Practice active listening, more complete responses to ideas you agree with (likes/concerns/wishes described in Aggressive Culture, above). Pay attention to your own areas of uncertainty and disclose them more readily. Recognize the need to pay attention to task, relationships, and your individual needs and wants. Learn about the behaviors that facilitate each of these elements and practice them in your interactions in the parish.

### Highest Candor with Highest Openness leads to a Collaborative Culture

Characterized by high trust, low turnover (although also likely to get a number of people who visit and decide not to join because they realize the parish isn't a good fit for them), and it is fairly easy to attract parishioners and staff.

The parish is very clear about what they are and what they aren't—there is good cultural fit among the organization, its leaders, and its members. There is high energy and creativity, a win/win mindset, and lower than average stress levels. The parish has a critical mass of competent and committed Christians. The primary task of the church is widely understood to be the formation of Christians and the renewal of baptismal identity.

### Examples of Collaborative Culture

The parish is an exciting, dynamic place to be. Parishioners are clear about baptismal identity and live into their apostolate at work, with friends and family, in the broader community, and at church. Things are happening based on organic energy and appropriate institutional support (little evidence of "we're doing this because we think we're supposed to" or begging for resources).

There is a strategic orientation—action takes place based on conscious attention to primary task. Parishioners are willing to identify and discuss parish initiatives, worship elements, or forms of decision making that appear to run counter to furtherance of the primary task.